D1217938

I AM HAUNTED

LIVING LIFE THROUGH THE DEAD

ZAK BAGANS

with KELLY CRIGGER

VB

VICTORY BELT PUBLISHING INC.

LAS VEGAS

First Published in 2015 by Victory Belt Publishing.

ISBN-13: 978-1-628600-61-2

This book is for entertainment purposes only. The publisher and authors of this book are not responsible in any manner whatsoever for any adverse effects arising directly or indirectly as a result of the information provided in this book. If not practiced safely and with caution, paranormal investigations can be hazardous to your health.

Interior and cover design by Yordan Terziev and Boryana Yordanova

Cover photo by Charles Henry

Printed in the U.S.A.

RRD 0115

I dedicate this book to all my amazing fans, my Ghost Adventures Crew (GAC) family, all my skeptics turned believers, and all the souls who have communicated with me and left a mark on my life forever.

THANK YOU:

My entire family for dealing with me and understanding the unique job and gift I have and that I'm not always myself when I return home from intense investigations

My dog, Gracie, and the Nevada SPCA

The spirits who have made contact with me and didn't harm me

My co-author, Kelly Crigger, for listening to my crazy stories and life every day

My publisher, Erich Krauss, and editor, Pam Mourouzis

My assistant, Cecilia Medina

Aaron Goodwin, Billy Tolley, Jay and Ashley Wasley, Bill Chappell, Dave Schrader, Devin Lawrence, Matthew Mourgides, Father Sebastiaan, Mark and Debby Constantino, Chris Fleming, Mike Haberman, Tara Bohren, Scott "Doctor" Gruenwald, Steve Barton, and Zory

And Harold the Haunted Doll for bruising my f-ing arm...I'll never pick you up again.

Contents

Introduction

They say that our life, our existence, contains more unknown than known. That must mean that in death we find out what the rest of the unknown is. I've traveled the world searching the darkest nooks and crannies of places only talked about in whispers—places most people fear to go. I've been through the ringer of emotions, from boundless joy to profound sorrow and paralyzing fear. I've stood on the edge of the abyss and faced death with an uncommon clarity. I've prodded and provoked things we don't understand in an effort to learn their secrets, in some cases hoping deep down inside that I wouldn't.

I've called out axe murderers, crawled through catacombs, been attacked by demons, been possessed by evil, and embarked on a quest to find the real Dracula. My adventures are a constant struggle between fear and courage. My body and soul bear the scars, but I consider myself fortunate. I made a conscious decision to do these things, and since 2004 my life has been a tumultuous journey through the best of times and the worst of times that I wouldn't trade for anything. People watch my TV shows and think they know me, but there are layers of my life that have never been made public.

Until now.

When you're young, life is just fun, but as you mature you learn to appreciate all the amazing things life has to offer. After all these years on the road, my experiences with the living and the dead have deepened my thinking and my overall sense of life. Life is beautiful. Life is horrific. Everything has its balance in the universe, and as I grow older, this balance is becoming clearer. I want to share it with you.

Some of the greatest books ever written are about the mysteries and discoveries of life on the road. Jack Kerouac, Paddy Fermor, and Hunter S. Thompson, to name a few, have given us the gift of venturing out into the world and looking at it in new and unexpected ways. The road is a lonely, exhausting, invigorating, and living thing, but the wonder of seeing things we never would have dreamed of makes it worth the price we pay to leave the safety of home.

If there's one thing I know, it's that I don't know enough. The question I most want to answer—what happens to us after death—is probably best left unanswered, when I think about it. It's the one mystery the universe will hold onto until we've all moved through it, and rightly so. Who are we to cheat death? The best we can hope for is to understand and manage it, and even that is pushing the boundaries of playing God. That doesn't mean I'll stop asking the question or searching for answers. I won't stop demanding to know more than we really should. I am human, after all. We humans are explorers and pioneers, and we find our inner strength when the end state is the absolute unknown.

In early 2014, Kelly Crigger and I decided to write a new book. We set up a system where I talked into my phone and sent him the files for transcription, and before long I found myself talking and talking and talking. I had more stuff to get off my chest than I realized; once the dam broke, I flooded the pages with stories of my life and adventures. But this is more than just a one-way conversation. I also learned a few things about myself. I've always known that I am haunted by the dead, but I didn't realize that I am also haunted by the living. As you're about to read, I have a distaste for modern society that tugs at my soul just as much as the spirits tug on me. We all grow up eventually, but being thrust into a white-hot spotlight of popularity turbocharged my maturation process. I have seen the best and worst in people both living and dead, and I want to share some of those experiences with you.

BUCKLE UP.

1

A Different State of Mind

Spirits and rituals have changed me.

Over the course of filming *Ghost Adventures*, I haven't matured just as a paranormal investigator and a TV personality, but as a person as well. My experiences have made me see the world differently than I did before this whirlwind of attention started. Before *GA*, I was what I would consider a normal guy—normal in the respect that I thought only about this material world. When I go out in public now, it seems that all I see is Madonna song material—people living in a material world. They do what society tells them to do. They have regular jobs and party on the weekends. They go to the movies at night. They spend money to get good-looking. That's the ebb and flow of present-day society. Those are the normal things people do. I'm not saying they're bad things, but as you've probably realized by now (or you will by the end of this book), I'm not normal.

I feel like I'm detaching from the material world. I don't know what's going on with me some days, but ever since I started filming *Ghost Adventures*, participating in rituals, communicating with the dead, and getting more serious about my work, my experiences have been more life-altering. Your typical paranormal investigator will go out and capture EVPs (electronic voice phenomena), do audio recordings and EMF (electromagnetic frequency) readings, take a few pictures, have a couple of experiences, see some shadows, and then go home, and they're back to their normal lives. That's not who I am. That's not what I'm all about. Every other week I'm at a new location getting deeper and deeper in touch with the spirit world.

When I look back at Nick Groff, Aaron Goodwin, and myself in the early days of the show, I see three guys who would do a lockdown but didn't have any idea what we were doing. We knew what we were supposed to do and what we felt we had to do in terms of our investigations, but we didn't know that much. Now we're in a deeper place, and at times I feel lost in the regular world, even though I have a lot of the things I always wanted, which I earned through hard work. I've been able to buy a nice house and cars and support myself without having to worry about paying bills. I earned that. For seven years I've delivered a number-one-rated TV show to a major network, along with many other successful projects. That's the American dream we all strive for: success and security.

So why do I still feel so lost?

Maybe it's because I've experienced things that I can't find easy answers to, and that makes me distance myself more and more from normal people who haven't seen the darkness. When I get home from an investigation or a lockdown, I don't want to be around anybody—not even my own family. I'm thinking about life, God, death, and what lies beyond as much as a young boy thinks about girls. It's on my mind 24/7, but it has consequences. I think about my interactions with spirits and the emotions I feel as a result, and at times I don't know whether I'm living or dying.

Don't get me wrong; I'm not depressed. It's more that being deeply in tune with a world that's dead is causing a shift in my life.

When you tap into a world that's bizarre, things can happen that no one understands. And then you belong to the spirits, not to yourself.

I see other paranormal investigators as people who are trying hard to figure out the basics of the spirit world, while I'm fully immersed in it. They're snorkeling in ten feet of water to look at the reef, while I'm at the bottom of the Mariana Trench. I'm in a very deep part of this field, and I don't mean in terms of evidence. That's what too many people focus on—visual, audio, visual, audio, audiovisual, EMF, EVP, proof, proof, proof. It never ends. There is proof, but it's more complicated than asking science to provide it. Science changes all the time, and what is accepted as true today can be disproved tomorrow.

Let's stop with the cliché that says, "There are no ghosts because science can't prove it." Those scientists will prove ghosts when they prove God. I've met dozens of skeptical scientists who don't believe in spirits or ghosts, yet they go to church every Sunday. There are just some things that can't be observed on cue and be put into a nice, neat box, so it's time to move on and admit that there are forces and worlds that far exceed what our minds can fathom. We should be looking for the *causes* of paranormal activity, not the effects. It's more advanced than any science experiment or what any human mind could possibly comprehend.

If you want to figure out the spirit world while you're alive, then beware—the deeper you get into it, the deeper they may want you, and the more powerful the pull is to find the answers. For some spirits and dark entities, it's one or the other—you stay in the living world and try to figure them out, or you join them to get the answers you're looking for. No living person has any solid answers about the spirit world. Everyone just has their own opinion. It's like religion. It's not proven; it's a belief. I've spent a lifetime discovering what I believe, and all I'm really sure of is that it's a dangerous place, especially when you take part in local rituals.

I've done several pagan rituals that called upon the ancient goddess of death, as well as a witchcraft ritual with a warlock who put a spell on us that we didn't even know about. Christian Day, a powerful warlock who legitimately knows rituals that awaken strange forces, told me to my face that he cursed me because he's mischievous. Nick, Aaron, and I participated in two rituals with Bloody Mary the Voodoo Queen, and Aaron went through nine months of hell afterward, which he believes was because of her.

These are powerful people who specialize in the summoning of spirits as part of their religion. And I don't know them that well. We're not friends, so I don't know if they're doing black magic on us to harm us or what. I don't know if these rituals have truly lifted a veil to reveal something evil, or if these people are trying to protect us from them. These people don't just go around doing rituals for entertainment, so when they do perform one, who's to say that they're not unleashing something even they can't control?

Paranormal investigators who don't participate in rituals or rely heavily on equipment-based investigation aren't doing all they can to find evidence, but that's okay, because not everyone should. I think it takes certain people who are more deeply connected to the spiritual world to successfully experiment and use rituals in order to knock on unfamiliar doors and establish a direct connection to the spirit world. We are equipment-based, but we have a balance. We're like the mixed martial arts fighters of PI. We're trained in scientific techniques, emotional connections, and historical research. I feel that few other paranormal investigators and TV shows (and let's be clear: I'm not talking down about anyone and respect other investigators and TV shows) go the extra mile to round out their skills. Conducting historical research and emotionally opening up to the energy of a location and the spirits found there are where we shine. To me, other investigators are relic hunters, like a guy on a beach with a metal detector. They know where they're going to go hunting, and that's one of the big differences right there: We don't hunt ghosts.

We don't call it ghost hunting even in jest. Ghost hunting is looking for something and using equipment to find it, and that defines these types of investigators. They're not using their own bodies and their own energy to their advantage. Although I disagree with them, I also understand why they decline to do it. They think the body is fallible and can give false responses, and therefore a disinterested, unemotional machine is a better tool to capture paranormal evidence. This is where our groups disagree. To me, the body is a perfectly reliable detector of paranormal energy if you know how to use it right to tune into the spiritual world. This is a defining difference between our group and others: our willingness to use our bodies as detectors and to try local spiritual and religious rituals. We harness the power of religious groups and practices and go beyond what cold science can prove or detect in terms of the existence of another dimension. We go as far as we can to lift the veil and open up a portal to make contact.

Think about it: If the spirit world is so much more advanced than the material world, then how can science and equipment go beyond known levels to detect it? I believe that EMF detectors and multispectrum camera equipment can do only so much. They can scratch the surface of the spirit world and catch a glimpse, like a shooting star in the desert, but can all that equipment capture anything when it's sitting still or turned off? No. It has to have a conduit to work. It has to be in the hands of a person asking questions of the ghosts. When you do that, you calibrate your energies and prepare the equipment for a peek through the Stargate and into the spirit world.

Equipment is great, but the emotional connection is indescribable. Your body is like a key trying to unlock a spiritual door. We're constantly opening ourselves up while we're using the equipment. Our results with the SB7 spirit box and every other piece of equipment we use are different because *we* are different from everybody else. When we go into a location together, Nick, Aaron, and I are like our own highly sophisticated piece of paranormal equipment.

I think our bodies are completely different from other investigators' bodies because we've spent years learning how to use them to detect spiritual energy and open doorways. We swim in the spiritual ocean while everyone else is snorkeling. I've never seen another paranormal show participate in a ritual. That's okay. Again, I'm not trying to speak ill of any other crew, but I don't think they're using all the tools in the toolbox to achieve their goals. We want to open ourselves up and open up those portals to make contact. Witchcraft, voodoo, paganism, cults…it's all good.

Is it dangerous? Absolutely. It's not an invitation to a birthday party; you never know what will come through once you open that door. We've had an evil creature growl at us from an altar in England after steam manifested from our mouths as a result of a 30-degree temperature drop, which made the witch conducting the ritual so afraid that she stopped the ceremony—something she'd never done in decades of conducting rituals. During a voodoo ritual, we captured a digital still photo of the most amazing phantom face in a trinity flame. "Bridget Bishop" (the first person executed for witchcraft during the Salem witch trials of 1692) gave us her first and last name during a ritual with a warlock and witch—eliciting one of the most priceless reactions by a third party in the history of our investigations.

It's risky, but if I feel that these spirits and rituals will do me harm, or if I have any indication that they're going to permanently damage my body or soul, will I stop? Yes. I have things that I want to do in this life. I've been through hell, I truly have. At one point I had nothing. I was totally lost because I couldn't do a 9-to-5 job. It was meaningless to me. I wasn't contributing to a bigger part of life, and I knew that there was something more inside me. I love what I do now more than anything else I can imagine.

Is it necessary to participate in rituals to try to find the secrets of the spirit world? I think it is. If you're not willing to face the danger to see what kind of responses you get, then you're not as serious as we are. These rituals have made us different people, but that's our choice. You have to have the passion to go further in this field. We're willing to take the risk, and that's what makes us different, but it has consequences.

As I grow older, I pay more attention to the effects of exposing myself to demons, evil spirits, and the most haunted locations around the world. Overdosing on energy while opening myself up to it and calling upon it, I see myself changing. I mean, who in his right mind would buy a Demon House while trying to heal mentally, physically, and spiritually from all the rituals, possessions, encounters, lockdown hangovers, and all the other stuff I've been through? Why buy a house that's said to be haunted by 200 demons that three different police officers and clergymen are scared of? Why not? It's like I'm trying to overdose on ghosts. I'm an addict.

Your average person won't go into a place full of negative energy for fear of attacks, attachments, channeling, possessions, or whatever, but I can't stop exploring them. I understand that my health is at risk. I understand that I'm being affected. I'm dealing with physical issues because of it. I'm dealing with mental issues because of it. I'm dealing with spiritual issues because of it. Yet I'm totally addicted to this field. I want that next big experience no matter what the cost.

Maybe that's why I'm bored with the material world. Everything is just stuff to me. Cars, houses, clubs, gambling…that's all it is here in Vegas. To me, a lot of this stuff is cool, but it's boring, too. I enjoy creating good memories with my family and friends. That's the part of life I like the most.

Most people have a preconceived notion of what life is and what is expected of them, but after seeing all the things I've seen and knowing what lies beyond this life, my attitude has changed. I'm not a slave to a schedule or to other people's expectations. People are so programmed by society, the tabloids, the Internet, and the like that they take the wrong things as truth and let themselves be puppets. They let the media tell them who's important until they find themselves worshipping the Kardashians and Bieber or who-ever's in the press this week. The Lords of Fame drive the herds of sheep. Every day you hear about their lives and who they're mar-rying or what they're drinking and…who the hell are they? What are they famous for? Paris Hilton, Kim Kardashian…what have they even done in life? Why are we supposed to obsess over these people? Why does the media force-feed us this bullshit instead of praising more worthy and talented people, like war heroes? Why do they treat untalented people like royalty? They have no backstory of overcoming adversity or accomplishing great things, yet they're hounded by the paparazzi and thrown in our faces every day.

I'm ranting, but I want to look beyond the greed, hate, and nega-tivity. I want to believe that there's a world without the deadly sins. Society is judgmental, and there are times when I don't want to be a part of it. I feel like I've been thrown into a river, and I just want to swim to the shore and get out. I stare back at the water and watch everyone go by yelling, "Jump in," but I don't want to. I want to stay on the shore and figure out what's hiding in the bushes. I'm not say-ing I want to die, but I do want to peer into the jungle and discover what's out there while everyone else floats by on inner tubes, bliss-fully unaware that they too will end up on the shore someday. We all do. Some of us will be more prepared than the rest.

When you venture off into uncharted areas, what will people do? They'll tell you, "No. You have to join us. You have to be part of society." Life moves fast, and I chose this field, so I can see what lies beyond it when it's done with me. Overexposure to the spirit world has made my thoughts deeper and clearer and my emotions much greater than I ever expected them to be.

TAKE MY HAND AND I'LL SHOW YOU.

2

MY CREW
IS MY FAMILY

Let me introduce you to
the people closest to me.

I've been on the road doing *Ghost Adventures* for seven years
nonstop.

Nonstop.

It's an exhausting life on all levels, but I wouldn't trade it for
anything. The show and the people who help me run it are a part
of me. Humans are social creatures, so nearly everyone has a family, a club, a crew, a union, a gang, a platoon, a church, a pack, or
some other sort of social entity to which they dedicate themselves.
The Ghost Adventures Crew is mine. I trust each and every one
of them completely, and when you give yourself to people on a
daily basis like that, you become very tight. Some days I have
to push myself that one extra yard just to make sure they're not
disappointed in me. That's what being us is all about. If you want
to know more about me, then you have to know the people who
surround me.

What a lot of people don't know is that I don't just host *Ghost
Adventures;* I am also the executive producer of the show. I make
the creative decisions and am in charge of all the other producers

and editors when we're not on set. At home, I work every single day on the rough edit until it's perfect. It never ends. I can't take any time off because we have deadlines for the network. So I'm either on the road or working all the time. This kind of pressure creates a special camaraderie between people—it's where a lifelong brotherhood is forged. A big reason why I can get through this insane schedule and hellish amount of travel (especially when I hate flying) is that I have great friends and family whom I don't just get along with, but truly enjoy being around.

Aaron is one of the most interesting people I've ever known, and I know a lot about him. Maybe too much. So how much can I say about this guy without him getting mad at me? He's a little more outrageous than me, so how about this analogy: If I'm an 8-year-old trapped in a 37-year-old body, then he's a 6-year-old trapped in a 38-year-old body. At some point we started calling each other G and talking in a slur just because…well, no reason, really. It seemed funny at the time, and somehow it stuck.

Aaron has ADD and can't sit still, which can be a pain in the ass sometimes because his mind never stops thinking and his body never stops moving. The guy has a lot of energy, and when you factor in his massive daily caffeine intake, it seems like you could put him on a treadmill and power Las Vegas. But it's a double-edged sword, because he can go from happy and laughing to Dark Aaron in a second. Dark Aaron can manifest like a demon with no warning. Dark Aaron is not a fun guy to be around, and when he comes out, I call him The Complainer. Dark Aaron complains about everything. None of us is perfect, but Dark Aaron could be in a hot tub with the Swedish bikini team and complain about the temperature. Dark Aaron can really drive me crazy when we're on the road and I've got a million tasks to accomplish and a show to run and the complaints pile onto an already huge mountain of stress. I've snapped and gone off on him, and we both end up apologizing and forgetting about it. Aaron and I have been through some shit together. We've almost tried to knock each other out, and we've cried together. And that's what makes us so close.

I love you to death, Aaron. You're my brother and one of my best friends, but I gotta let the fans know about that day in Denver. We'd just arrived, and Dark Aaron was in full force, for what reason I don't know. We were at a grill, and Aaron was quiet. Dark Aaron is like a dog that has rabies: You know it's happening and you keep your distance. As I was eating my dinner, my left elbow barely touched the bread on his plate. It was like an unintentional boob graze in a crowded bar that you immediately feel bad for. He responded with a nasty remark, and I wasn't in the mood. I'll just say that we had a moment when I recommended he change his attitude immediately. He ended up giving me the cold shoulder, and it made me want to beat up Dark Aaron to get Real Aaron back. Like I said, Real Aaron is a great person and my brother, and I've got his back no matter what, but Dark Aaron can dive back into the pit at Bobby Mackey's where he came from and stay there.

Aaron is also the pickiest eater I've ever met, and his quirks about restaurants would boggle the mind of Sigmund Freud. He's into examining food and every ingredient in it. He won't eat frozen hamburger patties (only fresh ones), or at places that use frozen hamburger patties that come from Sysco, or anything that contains corn syrup. He won't eat at Chipotle because they use corn oil. He won't eat at Subway because there's an ingredient in the bread that's also used to make yoga mats. He won't eat at McDonald's because they slash and burn half the Amazon rainforest to make grazing land for their cows. He will eat at maybe 30 percent of the restaurant chains in the U.S. As you can imagine, this makes it difficult when we all want to go out to eat, especially if we're in a backwoods location and the crew is starving. Aaron will skip out on us or hold out for as long as possible until something appealing comes along. You would think that we'd research our locations better so that Aaron could have pleasurable dining experiences, but that never happens. Someday I'll surprise him with a catered lockdown on his birthday.

When the crew comes together, we connect in a psychic triangle of energy that I truly believe opens up a portal for the spirits

I'm the best wingman.

to communicate with us and through us. I think our meeting back in 2003 was more than a coincidence. I believe that everything happens for a reason, and us meeting to make a documentary film is only one part of the big picture. I believe that something more powerful than us wanted us to meet and bring the paranormal into everyone's lives through the popular medium of TV.

Billy Tolley is a good guy. I met him about five years ago when he reached out to me on MySpace. He had an OCD-like obsession with EVPs, and his passion for getting into the mechanics of how they work was inspiring. The more I got to know him, the more I liked him. At the time, Billy was a Las Vegas club DJ, but he also did brilliant work with audio and video, so I saw a way to bring him in and eventually invited him to be a part of the Ghost Adventures Crew as a reviewer of evidence when we got home from lockdowns. He didn't travel with us at first, but he slowly became an integral part of the group and added a lot of value to what we did, so I eventually offered him a permanent spot on the show running the nerve center. That's how I do things. If people do good work and have the right attitude, then I promote them. Billy has been a great addition to the GAC and has become one of my best friends, like Aaron. The three of us talk and hang out every day when the cameras are off and we're at home in Vegas. Billy recently turned 41, so I give him a hard time for being old. It's not like he's 8 like me.

Our audio tech, Jay Wasley, and his wife, Ashley, are a big part of the production and also good friends. Jay is one of those guys who's always there when I'm having a health problem. If I'm not feeling well or something is freaking me out or making me feel depressed or like I'm going to die, Jay is there to help me through it. He's the guy who will come to my room or meet me somewhere to talk. There's not a bad bone in his body; he's as genuine and compassionate as they come. So I do whatever I can for the guy, like promoting him from production audio to audiovisual tech on camera (yes, there's a difference).

Jay is a fascinating person. I give nicknames to everyone on the crew, and I call Jay The Theorist because whenever we're having off-camera talks, he comes up with these crazy theories on things, like "coffee beans make the hair on your head crystallize into aromatherapy and get rid of migraine headaches." Dude...what? He's also very valuable while we're filming because he reads a lot and is very intelligent. I can be talking, interviewing, or hosting the show, and Jay will pop up out of nowhere with an awesome piece of research that's relevant to what I'm doing and really adds to the production. He's like Alex Trebek on speed.

Case in point: We were investigating the Pioneer Saloon in Goodsprings, Nevada. During lockdown, a woman's voice came through the spirit box and gave us her unusual name. As soon as he heard it in the nerve center, Jay got on the phone, searched the census reports from the nineteenth century, and found this woman's name, so we knew what spirit we were dealing with. That's the kind of quick wit and dedication that makes the show better. Plus, he's never in a bad mood, and you'll never hear him argue with anyone, so he's great to have around...except for his diet. He eats the weirdest vegetarian stuff that I can't even identify.

Jay's wife, Ashley, is our still photographer, and she comes along on every shoot. During the first two days at any location, Ashley takes still photos of us while we're doing interviews, researching the location, getting B-roll footage, setting up, or whatever. All her photos get uploaded to TravelChannel.com, and she's definitely a part of the GAC inner circle. I'm weird about who I consider to be in the inner circle of the production crew, but the Wasleys, who are modern-day hippies in a way, are awesome. I could see them driving an old VW bus.

Laughter is so important. I'm dedicated, driven, and passionate about what I do, and I control my world very tightly, but if you can't give your friends a hard time and then laugh about it, then they're not really your friends, or you're in a bad situation that needs to change. We rag on each other all the time and just laugh it off. It alleviates the pressures and stresses of doing what we do. That's the thing about us: When we're not filming, or when I'm not under the intense pressure of doing an investigation and delivering a great TV show as the producer and/or director, we let loose. When I'm not *that* Zak, I'm the goofy Zak—the kid-trapped-in-an-adult's-body Zak. Within our core family, we joke

My crew is my family.

around a lot, make stupid Vine videos, tweet to each other, and talk in our own silly language on the set. The demands of our job and the constant travel are difficult, but having a family on the road that you can be yourself around is a huge benefit of being a part of the GAC, and a big relief. We can talk about anything around each other; that's just how we are.

When you live on the road as much as we do, with such a big group, you get to know them whether you want to or not. At times they drive you crazy, and at other times you can't live without them. If one of us isn't feeling well or is in a bad mood, the others pick up the slack. We're a great big dysfunctional family that works well together whether we're on set or off.

I think the world would be a better place if everyone had this kind of tight-knit support system. For the most part, humans are not lone wolves, but pack animals. We congregate in groups, identify with those groups, and make sacrifices for those groups. Whether it's a hockey team, a police squad, or a firefighting crew, the people you work hard with become your family, and that's certainly true of the GAC.

**THAT'S WHAT MAKES IT SO REWARDING:
THE PEOPLE.**

3
THE DEMON HOUSE

One kid walks backward up a
wall and the world goes crazy.

It was January 2014, and I was in San Pedro, California, when my cell phone blew up. Hundreds of emails, tweets, and text messages began pouring in about a family in Gary, Indiana, that was possessed by a demon. Their house was allegedly infested. The story had just broken in the *Indianapolis Star,* and a lot of people wanted to bring it to my attention. The sheer volume of people reaching out to me was the first red flag of many to come about this place, so I was immediately intrigued.

I've read about and investigated many demonic possessions, but this one was different. A lot of people you wouldn't expect to come forward—police officers, state officials, nurses, doctors, and psychologists—had witnessed supernatural phenomena with this possession and seemed to change from skeptics to believers overnight. People had experiences both inside and outside the house, the most profound of which was a boy walking backward up a wall in a nearby hospital emergency room.

Something drew me to this story, and not just a little, but a lot. I was completely engrossed. As I was getting ready to hit my call time to film an episode of *Ghost Adventures,* I couldn't get the story out of my mind. I wanted to investigate, but I knew right away that there would be a conflict. The story had already gone public, and being a TV show host, I knew that the entertainment industry would be all over it. Stories like this, especially when they're true or backed by real events, are like crack cocaine for Hollywood. The story practically writes itself, and it has a built-in audience in the people who have been following along. The competition would be stiff.

My first thought was to make a documentary film about what had happened in the house and to the family, because documentary filmmaking is my passion. (My 2006 documentary film *Ghost Adventures* is how I got into this business in the first place.) But there was something more here. This story is bigger than just me and a documentary film. It could help provide answers to some of the oldest mysteries of the paranormal world, so I wanted to be a part of it. It's like an astrophysicist finding out that a huge meteor has just hit Indiana, and there are fragments of it all over the state. It's what the astrophysicist has been looking for his whole life, and suddenly it's in Indiana. So to me, getting involved was not a want, but a *need.* It was one of the most credible and witnessed demonic possessions I've ever heard about in the media, and I had to get involved.

I hadn't made a documentary film since 2006, and this project had a lot of great facets to it: a great story, public interest, and an unexplained paranormal phenomenon. It wasn't about the money or about exploiting anyone. I wanted to be part of a historic paranormal event, and there was no way I was going to be stopped.

The first thing I did was call my golden connection, Dave Schrader. Dave and I have worked together on many projects, including *Paranormal Challenge,* Darkness Radio, and Coast to

Coast Radio. He's a great person to network with, and he quickly got me in touch with the priest in this case, Father Michael Maginot. His name was in the headlines, so he's the first guy I called. We talked for half an hour. I told him who I was and that I was interested in doing a film about the true events that had taken place there. He assured me that he was interested in doing a film with me, but nothing was in writing, which made me nervous because I knew that 500 people were going to be calling him. It was a headline on every major news outlet around the world, so I knew I was fighting everyone for the story: paranormal people, TV people, film producers, you name it. All the sharks would be circling. The family to whom all this had happened put up a big wall, too. After the story broke, they weren't taking calls.

Then I had an idea. While everyone else was trying to get to the family, the priest, the ER staff, and the reporter who broke the story in the Indiana press, I decided to go a different route and get into the house itself. A house in which a demonic possession takes place is sacred in our profession, so I figured if I bought the house, then I could investigate it whenever I wanted and figure out what was happening on my own terms. I'm fortunate to have made a decent living from my TV shows, so maybe I could pull out a trump card that no one else could and make the house mine. That would be a huge victory.

But there was a problem: In order to buy the house, I needed to find the owner, Charles Reed. I remembered seeing him in one of the videos about the incident, but how could I find him? The house had been rented to a new family, and I couldn't go through them— they didn't like all the attention and were angry about the media trying to get close.

After several unsuccessful attempts to get a hold of Reed, my buddy Dave Schrader came through again with Reed's cell phone number, so I called and left a message. (All this was happening just before my call time to film *Ghost Adventures,* mind you.) Minutes later, my phone rang, and it was him.

YES!

But now I had to tell this guy that I wanted to buy his house on the spot, even though it wasn't for sale. So I explained who I was, and I thought to myself, *Just get to the point.* I blurted it out: "Hey, man, I saw your house on the news this morning, and I want to buy it." I held my breath for a split second. Would he be offended? Would he want a kajillion dollars for it? Would he hang up?

"Sure," he said. "How much?"

That was the best feeling in the world. I didn't spit out a number because I had no idea what the Indiana real estate market was like. Instead, I left it to him to start the bidding.

"Thirty-five thousand," he said.

"Deal!" I sent him a PayPal deposit minutes later and went to film my episode, the sweet smell of victory radiating off of me.

But the next day I began to worry. I thought the media blitz might make Reed think that he could get more money from someone else, and our verbal contract wasn't going to hold up. I wasn't trying to steal the house from him. He told me the asking price and I agreed, so it should be all good, right? I called him back and asked him to send me an email stating that I had bought the house and he had received the deposit, which he did. That made me feel better.

So I had my foot in the door—literally. The house was mine. At this point, it wasn't so much about making a film as it was about getting into the house and investigating it for myself. I had to see the forces at work in Indiana that had caused such an uproar. But it's never that easy, is it?

Somehow word spread that I'd bought the house, even though the transaction between Reed and me was private. Marisa Kwiatkowski, the reporter who broke the story for the *Indianapolis Star,* called me, asked for details, and asked if she could publish them. I was shocked at how quickly she'd learned about the purchase, but I said yes. I wasn't trying to hide anything, so why not? Her article came out the next morning, and I was flooded with media requests like never before. Seriously, I've never had so much media attention in my life, from Germany to Australia to every news source in the U.S. The home page of the *USA Today* website reported that I had bought the "Demon House" and planned on doing an investigation and possibly a documentary or feature film, and with that article came a lot of interview requests.

I was asked to be on *Inside Edition* twice, and I did those interviews back at home in Las Vegas. During the interviews, I explained why I had bought the house and what it meant to me. Because of the number of credible witnesses who had seen supernatural things, including three police officers (from three separate jurisdictions) who had witnessed events that had made them believers, I couldn't resist being a part of it.

A demonic possession is a fight between good and evil over a human soul. When an exorcism is conducted, a priest fights with the devil for the human being who's infected. We can learn a lot from these exorcisms.

Religion is taught through sacred texts like the Bible. But for atheists and nonbelievers, the Bible is still a book, and it's the story of Jesus Christ, a man. He's not here to sit down and tell us that everything ever written about Him is true. Having faith means believing in his teachings, which have been passed down through many generations. And people believe in different gods. Christianity, Judaism, Islam—these are all belief systems, and they are different for everyone. But an exorcism that involves supernatural events that defy the laws of physics and scientific explanation…I believe something godlike is connected to this event. At the very least, there's a force at work that we don't understand, but should strive to. To me, this is the crux of being a paranormal investigator. A lot of people don't believe in anything they can't see or feel, so a possession is a way we can see God and the devil and justify our religious beliefs. Many find it scary and want to get away from it or deny it. But I want to be there to document it and learn from it, like a storm-chaser rushing to the next killer tornado. I want to find proof that there's something more than a living physical body that can also exist on the other side. It would give us answers to so many things we don't understand yet about life, the afterlife, God, you name it.

There's a big risk that goes along with all this: We don't understand what we're messing with. The highest members of the clergy can't tell us exactly who God is or how He came to exist. There are theories and scriptures, but to actually witness God defeating the devil in an exorcism…I think that's the most powerful material event in the living world that lets us witness the power of God. It's more powerful than prayer. In prayer, you wait for a response. There's no beam of light while you're praying (that I know of) that shoots down and enables you to talk face-to-face with God. People who want to feel God go to church and raise their hands to get a closer connection to Him. Sometimes they think they feel him (and some people might), but there are more mysteries surrounding God than anything. But in an exorcism, you can actually do that: feel the power of God.

It's what I think combat must be like when an enemy soldier gets shot. When the bullets hit the enemy, you see the effect it has on him. In an exorcism, when a priest says the words of God, it's like bullets hitting the demon and terminating it. It's proof to me that the power of God is real. Seeing exorcisms work has made me more religious. And I'm intrigued by holy water burning the skin and a cross debilitating a demon. It goes much deeper than ghost hunting for me. We're getting at the source of spirits and the afterlife.

So I owned the house and was doing a bunch of interviews. In a way it was good to have my name in the media, because the family, the priest, the police officers, and everyone else who had witnessed these events saw that I was serious about getting to the bottom of what had happened. It kind of put them in shock, too, because the press associated them with me in a lot of articles. That should have made it easy for me to get a hold of them and learn their stories, right?

Nope. I did everything I could think of to contact them and got nowhere. Only Father Michael, the priest who had performed the exorcism, would talk to me. He even thought it was great that I had bought the house. So I sent him an exclusive agreement to make a documentary film, which he signed. Owning the rights to his story was a huge coup, so I decided not to wait and to make the film immediately.

I hired Matt Mourgides to be my production manager, some camera crewmen from LA, and Jay Wasley and Billy Tolley for electronics. While we were in pre-production, my main focus was to interview everyone who had been involved as quickly as possible, before any sharks could lock them up and steal them away from me.

Right away I had an issue. (The obstacles to this project never stop popping up.) I was contacted by a producer who said that he had worked on a paranormal movie. Our conversation was very vague at first. I didn't want to play my hand, so I left things open until I could figure out his angle. He said that he loved my story about buying the house and wanted to talk again later, so I hung up thinking nothing more about it. But it wouldn't be the last time I would hear from him.

I went back to making my film and quickly learned that everyone's ego had swollen since the story broke. So much attention was being paid to the people involved that they started shopping their stories around to the highest bidder. This is America, and I get it, but it was frustrating nonetheless. Everyone was hard to talk to. The *Indianapolis Star* wouldn't let me use Marisa's articles in the film, and I wasn't allowed to interview her. She offered to meet me at the house to have the *Star* write about my making the documentary, but it doesn't work that way. This is a two-way street: You help me and I help you. They gave me all this attention for buying the house but then wouldn't allow me the courtesy of an interview or give me permission to use her article in the film, so I flushed that plan.

Next up was Captain Charles Austin of the Gary Police Department, who was one of the first officers to respond to the family. He had investigated along with Child Protective Services because the kids were going to school with bloody noses and not acting right. CPS took the kids away and went to the home with Captain Austin to interview the family. This is when they told them that they were possessed by demons, and Captain Austin didn't believe them for a second. He thought they were making it up, and can you blame him? But then he had his own experience. After walking back to his police car to drive away, his AM/FM radio came to life with very high static, and a deep, demonic voice came through saying, "YOU IN THERE!" He was on the phone with another police officer back at the Demon House when it happened, and the other officer heard the voice, too. That officer also saw an apparition in the house, so suddenly the police believed the family's claims of demonic possession because they saw it themselves! Later, Captain Austin would label the house "a portal to hell."

I talked with Captain Austin, and, man, is he a character. He's funny, laughs a lot, and is a pleasure to be around. One day, he told me that another producer had contacted him. It turned out to be a guy I know, which shows you how competitive the entertainment industry is. Everyone was going after these people—including me, to be honest, but there was a difference in our objectives. Hollywood sees the money in the story, and I just want to tell the story. My production isn't designed for maximum profit; it's bare bones so I can capture what happened. After talking with Charles Austin many times, I got the impression that he would give me an on-camera interview, as would the landlord. At that point I had a filming schedule, a crew, a lot of equipment, three of the participants, and the house. Ultimately the family was the priority, but no one had heard from them, probably because everyone wanted the life rights to their story. I couldn't compete with the offers that I knew were being tossed at them anyway.

Inside Edition wanted to do another interview with me in the house, but I wasn't sure because I hadn't done a proper investigation yet. We were in our third or fourth day of filming background shots and superficial pieces, and at one point something dark happened. I think I saw a demon attack someone I let into the house. It shocked me and the crew. I had no idea what was waiting for us in that house, so there was no way I was going to let reporters in. Besides, it would have been irresponsible of me to give them access when I knew that there was a risk of bodily harm. I might as well have invited them to go over Niagara Falls in a barrel.

So I kept *Inside Edition* on the porch and did an interview with them there, and right away I wasn't feeling well. Not myself at all. I didn't know if I was sick, tired, or what, but I was foggy and unable to concentrate. It felt like everyone was speaking in slow motion. I didn't want to be there, but I kept telling myself to be professional and fight through it. You can Google that interview and see how out of it I was. Later, the crew told me that I was different every time we went to that place. Even if we were just putting in a smoke detector or walking around, I seemed to get meaner and more short-tempered. I've been around a lot of bad energy and I've fought with a few nasty demons, but this place was different—so much that it actually made me stop filming for a while.

One day we were troubleshooting a camera system. No filming was going on except for the surveillance cameras, when I suddenly went off on a crew member for no reason. I was shouting at him, and things got physical. This man weighs 200 pounds, and I picked him up and pinned him against a wall, something I'm not sure I

Doing an interview with *Inside Edition* at the Demon House.

could do on my own. Later he said that I seemed to have superhuman strength and didn't look like myself when it happened.

So many things have happened to people in that house—workers removing mold, plumbers, the building inspector, everyone has some type of experience while they're there or after they leave. Strange things even happened to people I interviewed for the documentary after they left the house.

To be honest, I feared for my life a few times there. Something kept telling me that I had to do this, but I don't want to sustain permanent damage. There's something about the house that I've connected with, for better or worse. After I pinned that guy up against the wall, I wanted to leave, but I didn't want to leave. I remember being at the front door looking back inside and seeing a tall, dark figure standing at the threshold of the kitchen leading down to the basement—the same type of figure the police officers saw. This is beyond anything I'd ever witnessed before. This is beyond the power of human spirits. This house may not be a portal to hell, but it's a portal to something that is powerful and evil.

At that point, I don't think I realized what I had gotten myself into. For most investigations, I can show up, do my job, come into contact with human spirits, go home, have a lockdown hangover for a day or two, and I'm fine. This place is different. It's indescribable. Something in this house is aware of me and uses me. An incident that occurred a few weeks later confirmed this belief.

A woman who claims to have lived in the house in the 1980s saw me on the news and reached out to my producers. After we validated that she had in fact lived there as a teen, we agreed to meet her at the house. She wanted to go inside, but I was hesitant. It was an open investigation where bad things had happened to children, and this woman had her family with her. It was dangerous, but she was insistent. She had lived there for many years, so finally I caved, and we all went in together. At first it seemed harmless. She showed me which room was hers, and we spent some time talking about what it had been like to live there. She even revealed that she'd had nightmares as a kid, and when she had a specific nightmare, someone she knew would die the next day. I honestly wasn't surprised given how evil this place is.

Then we headed downstairs to the basement, but as we moved through it, something happened to the woman's leg, like something hit her or a dog bit it. She said, "Ow!" and turned to her son to yell at him, but he was ten feet away and had nothing to do with it. She was angry. "Why the hell did you do that?" she spat. It was a strange moment, and she immediately went upstairs and left the house. The visit pretty much ended right there.

Days later, she called to say that her daughter was possessed and hadn't been the same since being in the house. Apparently her daughter tried to kill herself and her mom just a few days after I met them, an act that was totally unlike her. Even worse was that she called me from the ER in Indianapolis, where her daughter was still being treated for a suicide attempt.

This was it for me—a punch in the gut, a slap in the face, and a kick in the crotch all at once. I was in deep. Really deep. I'd bought a portal to hell that had some sort of guard dog demon prowling around it, and it shook my self-confidence. It's like deciding to hang out with a bad crowd and seeing them do bad things and knowing you don't belong there. Your first instinct is to look for a way out.

But then I remembered that I was stronger than that. I had to be there. I had to do this. I had to see what was going on in this house and document it. I felt responsible for allowing these innocent people into the house, and I'll never be able to take that back, but I could make it right, too. I could fight the darkness that had set up this awful situation. It was the demon's will. It persuaded me to let a new family into the house so that it could do damage to them, and I wasn't strong enough to stop it. Well, that won't happen again. I bought this portal to hell, and it's too late to get my money back, so I'm all in. There are no refunds when it comes to fighting evil.

But the challenges are constant. Around this time I discovered that Father Mike had signed a contract with another producer (just four days after signing one with me), and it hit the media immediately. So I called him and reminded him that he had signed an exclusive agreement with me, and that exclusivity was implicitly outlined. He said that he wanted to do a documentary with me and a Hollywood feature film with the other guy, and he didn't see a problem with doing both. I explained that he couldn't. There's more legal information that I can't write about, but the point is that he signed a contract to be a part of my movie and also wanted to be part of a separate movie, which was a violation of my contract.

Father Mike and I had a good talk, but suddenly I got a call from that other producer while I was at the house. He immediately said that I'd better watch it because I didn't know what I was getting myself into, which I took as a threat. He belittled me over and over again on the phone and tried to bully me to get me out of the picture. He kept throwing out the amount of money that his movie had made to make me feel small, but it had the opposite effect. I hung up the phone and dug my heels in for a fight. Money changes people, and I can say that with the benefit of experience on my side. This guy threw his money around like it was morals and he was a better person than me because he had more. That logic doesn't work. That's like saying the sun revolves around the Earth. I suddenly felt like I was in a different movie, where I was the protagonist trying to tell the story while a big-money antagonist tried to stop me. I wasn't flinching.

You have to be extremely dedicated to your story as a documentary filmmaker. You have to be constantly aware of new developments. You have to learn how to pursue those developments and find an ending that helps explain or expands on the original story. It's those different canals that lead off of the main river that add interest and credibility instead of telling the same story that everyone's already heard. You run into obstacles and barriers, and you have to get through them to get what you want. When you do, you gain respect as a filmmaker. Not everyone has the tenacity to make a great film.

The barriers that have been thrown in front of me since I bought the Demon House have been incredible. I feel like an Amazon explorer trapping a new, unknown spider that everyone wants to see, but I can't let them see it until I know what it can do. *Inside Edition* pressured me over and over again to get inside the house because they wanted to be the first to take cameras in. But I'd just witnessed something extraordinary, and since I owned the house, I knew I'd be putting their camera crew in jeopardy if I let them in.

As I write this book, I'm midway through filming my documentary about the house. There are so many more things that have happened that I want to talk about, and so many more details that I'd like to share, but it's complex…and dangerous.

LOOK FOR *THE DEMON HOUSE* MOVIE TO COME OUT IN 2015.

4

My Oasis in the Desert

Getting away is a necessity.

In the days leading up to a lockdown, we do a lot of preparation and talk to a lot of people. When we filmed in Pioche, Nevada, I spoke with a few old-timers who lived there and found each of their stories to be similar to mine. One used to live in Las Vegas and had escaped to this old mining town because life was simpler there, and another was slowly being overtaken by disease and wanted to spend the rest of his days away from the noise of society. At times like these, I find myself face-to-face with who I may become when the time is right.

There are only a couple hundred people living in Pioche today. It's one of those communities where everyone gathers around a grill and the old fire truck drives in with Santa riding high atop it for the kids at Christmas. It's those simple pleasures of life that I pine for, preserved in Norman Rockwell style in these little towns that time has turned a blind eye to.

I'm not saying that Pioche is a perfect, idyllic place, but it is far less noisy and pretentious than mainstream America, and I always seem to be drawn to these types of towns. People who live in towns

44

like these don't obsess over Bieber and the Kardashians, and the local press is more concerned with relevant civic issues than with worshipping pop stars and socialites.

This day and age makes me sick sometimes. It's disgusting and selfish in so many ways that it drives me to separate from it. That's one reason I love traveling: It gives me the chance to escape into these nooks and crannies of space and time. But my experience is always a little different from everyone else's. Being a sensitive and an empath, I'm not just visiting an old town looking at rundown buildings; I can actually feel the spirits and their energy. If you put a blindfold on me, put me in a van, and drop me off in a town like Pioche, I can instantly feel that I'm in a different time. It's a therapeutic escape that I miss after the shoot is over and I'm back in loud, neon Vegas. Traveling to these places off the beaten path is my privilege and my sanctuary. I'm definitely a guy who prefers the road less traveled.

This temporary release from the noise of society is one reason I keep making *Ghost Adventures.* It's a serene island in an ocean of chaos. Everyone wishes they could go back in time and feel what it was like to live in a different world—at least temporarily. We all enjoy the comforts of modern life, like medicine, transportation, electricity, and running water, and I have to admit that I'm no different.

Some of my favorite spots to film are old Wild West mining towns in the desert. I've been all over Nevada and the Southwest and have swallowed more than my fair share of dust. But the more desolate a place is, the more I enjoy it. Bannack Ghost Town in Montana is beautiful. Historic old towns like Gettysburg are insanely cool to me as well. I love a location with a good story, and the Colonial East Coast has a ton of stories to tell. On set, I'm no longer in 2014; I'm in the eighteenth or nineteenth century. I wear my cowboy hat and boots or whatever the location calls for, and for three days I'm truly free. I'm not famous or successful, just a guy doing his job, and at times I wish I could stay there. In these ghost towns, I'll sit in an old rocking chair and observe the people who live there. Many look like they've been through hell but are peacefully riding out the rest of their days in solitude. Some days I want that for myself, too.

On the flip side, I also need an element of adventure, in case I get a little bored. The murders, suicides, abductions, scandals, and mysteries that built these towns are spellbinding to me. I've always found the dead more interesting than the living because they have more secrets to discover. I can talk to a living person today and learn their secrets pretty quickly, but the dead are tough nuts to crack. They lived in a different time with different lifestyles and even different speech. We sometimes think of them as rudimentary or simple people, but really they weren't. They had the same problems we do, but different ways of dealing with them. That's intriguing to me.

When I travel to these towns, there are always mysteries to unravel. I can go back in time and pick up a cold case murder and try to ask the victim what happened. Communicating with spirits from the past is a true adventure. I get to meet the people of that era and area and see how different they were. Some say that the people create the environment, but after all my travels, I think it's the other way around—the environment shapes the people. Those who live in a dirty place tend to be meaner, less trustworthy, and more violent. People who are brought up in a nicer place are likely to have better manners and care more about helping others. This is a generalization, of course, but I've observed a lot of people and find it to be true a lot of the time.

Many people are stuck in a bad environment or situation that they can't get away from. I was stuck in Detroit for years and kept telling myself that if I just made a little more money, I could leave. It was a miserable time because I never found my place there. There was no purpose to any of the jobs I held. I would go home and then go through the same meaningless stuff again the next day. I had no impact on people. There was no adventure. I wasn't dissecting life

I love the ol' west. I've been here before, just not in this life.

to uncover its mysteries. That's how I wanted to live, but I wasn't sure how to accomplish it.

As a kid, I used to fear that my life would be wasted. I would agonize over how I was going to live this finite life. We have only so much time, after all, and I didn't want my only experiences with different cultures to be on TV or in the pages of *National Geographic.* I wanted to visit the Kansas plains, the Virginia battle-fields, and the California coast. I wanted to see the world instead of being stuck in just one part of it. I wanted to feel the energies of new places and different people, and I wanted to experience the glories of history. But as I get older, I can see the benefits of settling down in a small town where you know everyone and become part of the lore. I absorb energy like a sponge everywhere I go. It allows me to see the world and my purpose in it. I wish everyone could do that. I wish everyone could see more than where they are today, and see how vast and wonderful the wide world is while also appreciating the beauty of the little corners.

The guy in Pioche who escaped Vegas said that he was running from something. I don't remember what it was (or maybe I just don't want to give his secret away), but he was seeking peace in this small town.

MAYBE I'M THE SAME.

5

DEEPER CONNECTION

Sometimes I zone out like
Walter Mitty, and that's not always
a good thing.

You know that old saying, "Be careful what you wish for, because you might get it"? Some days that's me. I walk through the paranormal door to discover all I can about the spirit world, and I develop a deep connection to the other side that sometimes overtakes me completely, whether I want it to or not. After a paranormal investigation, I seem to have a residual connection with the spirits that I don't know about until days, weeks, or even months later...when *they* want to make contact, not the other way around. It's almost like being kidnapped, or at least forced to go somewhere and listen to something regardless of how you feel about it. I worked hard to open a door, but now I can't shut it.

Recently I was driving home from my mom's house through Las Vegas, and at a stoplight I was suddenly transported back to La Purisma Mission in Lompoc, California, one of the first investigations we did for *Ghost Adventures*. It had been the site of some pretty barbaric events, and the spirit energy was so strong there that it stayed with me, but I never knew that it would someday take hold of my mind. While my car was stopped at this light, I was back in the eighteenth century, sitting around a campfire with the women and children of the Chumash Indians. Everyone was laughing and happy. I was there, really there. It was as if I had gone back in time at a Vegas stoplight, of all places. It was so vivid that I couldn't shrug it off as a simple flashback.

These reflections from past investigations float in and out of my life like the flute music we captured on the tribal grounds. I feel as though a part of me stayed with the spirits there, and at certain moments those spirits can call upon me and demand that I listen. They can still communicate through me. They seek relief from their pain by igniting visions within me. I get so deep into these visions that it's hard to break free. At that stoplight, I was back in the 1700s. It was a sunny day. The women were making pottery. The children were playing and having a good time. I could feel every bit of it, and I had to force my hand to reach forward and turn on some music just to get myself straight enough to drive home.

La Purisma isn't the only example. I get it from all the places I go. The spirits select me, and I never know which ones are going to come and when. In certain locations I can almost transport myself back in time to those moments we're investigating. At Gettysburg, for example, I could smell the sulfur and death in the air and see the sun shining on the scorched battlefield in July 1863. I could hear the screams of the men having their legs sawed off. Long after I left the battlefield, I felt the pain of bullets hitting a soldier in the chest and fell to the floor in agony as he would have fallen as he took his last breath.

One time I was at home relaxing in a chair and *boom*—I was in a recliner at Waverly Hills Sanitarium with the other patients who were dying of tuberculosis. We were on the breezeway, where the terminally ill spent their days. There was a woman with curly hair. I believe it was the one whose picture was on the wall there—the one I left flowers for. I shared comforting stories with this woman before she died.

I don't know what it is, but it seems like a part of me gets left behind at these locations, and the spirits can find me through that. It sounds crazy, but these episodes are happening more and more often now, and they're more powerful every time, which makes me wonder if they'll ever get so strong that I won't be able to get myself back. Will I pass out on the floor and be trapped in another time while doctors try to figure out what's wrong with me, and eventually call it something they understand, like a stroke?

Many times it's stronger than just a vision, and my emotions are part of the experience. I really feel that it's an ethereal connection that I made during the investigation by opening myself up to the spirits. It's almost like I'm transplanting or channeling them through me and me through them, but it's stored deep inside me and comes out only at certain moments.

You could say that I'm a human satellite. The spirits reach out to me because they know I have a good heart and a good soul. They know I was sent there for more than a TV show. It's my destiny and my fate. In the beginning, I was more focused on taunting evil spirits and enticing them into a fight, but now I feel like I do more. I help people, but I also help spirits.

When you have a family member who's in pain, what do you do? You talk to them and show through your empathy that you're also in pain. You comfort them with words and touch and let them sense that you're hurting, too, which relieves them. That's what I do for these spirits. I don't just help them; I also guide them through the astral plane. We humans are constantly striving for happiness, so is it so hard to imagine that spirits who were once human would want the same thing? We all want to be free of pain, disease, violence, and suffering. Life is a fight against these adversities. Even when

we're happy, we fear falling toward a state of illness, trauma, insecurity, or whatever.

Most of the places I've investigated have been the sites of atrocities and disasters that resulted in pain, suffering, and death. These places are vortexes of supercharged emotion, and I believe that the physical surroundings—the trees, the rocks, the walls—can hold onto the energy of those disasters. But more incredibly, so do I, and I frequently experience delayed pain from making contact with spirits. I'm sure we all try to avoid death, but I believe it's this moment of mortality when a person dies that imprints a spirit on its surroundings and keeps some spirits earthbound because they're still fighting to get their lives back. Wouldn't any of us do the same?

When I'm not filming, I don't go out a lot anymore. I'm not around people as much as I used to be. I don't leave my house like I did a few years ago. Instead, I travel back to the places I've been to visit the spirits there; even though I'm physically at my house, my mind is always away. I visit these spirits just like you would visit your friends. Usually I see smiles and happiness, which I'd like to think is because I came to see them. I know how strange this sounds, but I don't care. I know it's real.

I deal with the world of the unknown and the unexplained. I can't explain why these things happen to me, but they do. All I can do is welcome it and try to learn from it. But I also worry that something darker may be aware that I'm involved in it. Am I making things worse by opening myself up?

I had a friend who had something dark come through while he was opening himself up to a loving spirit. He's smart, educated, and likable, but he was not aware that something evil could find him. He was so focused on opening up to a good spirit with love and compassion that he never saw the dark one that blindsided him. Your soul is like the Stargate. If you open it up too long to the spirit world, bad things can come through, and they'll attach themselves to you. His sessions with the loving spirit were too long and too open, and he was unprepared for what could happen. His armor wasn't strong enough to combat anything dark. His emotions were focused on the good things, and that left him vulnerable to the bad thing that came through and still affects him to this day.

Dark things have tried to come for me, but I'm always ready for them. I train myself and my soul to be strong while I visit other times and spirits. I gain knowledge from others in the field: parapsychologists, psychic mediums, and demonologists. I prepare and cleanse myself with prayer, meditation, and communing with Mother Nature. If you try to contact spirits without doing those things first, something bad will take notice and try to destroy you. The more you work in and around the paranormal, the more you open yourself up to the dark side of it, which is dangerous. You're vulnerable to paranormal diseases that you can't get rid of. This isn't the thrill ride that many people think it is. There are health risks and life-or-death situations that most people don't understand.

I don't fear the visions I have because most of them are sad or happy and pretty nonthreatening. However, some are evil, and those are the ones that concern me. One such episode shook me to the core.

I usually get visions in the daytime, but of course we all dream. One night I dreamed that I had powers. I was a ghost with the ability to move things. I was at a bar and made a glass slide into my hand like a parlor trick. The next thing I knew, a giant satanic creature with hooves and backward antlers was standing in front of me. Then he had control of me. I was frozen as he opened his mouth and mine opened at the same time, against my will. Smoke came out of his mouth that I was inhaling, and then suddenly I woke up. I was shaken, but I got over it.

Fast-forward a few months. I hadn't told anyone about that dream, and out of the blue I got a text from Chris Fleming, a psychic medium and friend. He'd heard that I bought the Demon House and wanted me to be careful because there was a satanic creature with hooves and backward horns in the house that was aware of me. I was chilled like never before. How could he have known? "I just know," he told me. He's done things like this in the past and is always spot on, so I heeded his advice when I finally set foot in that place.

In addition to my connection to the dead, I'm gifted with the ability to connect with the living on a deeper level. I am an empath, meaning that I can feel the emotions of others near me. From a young age I've had a hypersensitivity to others' emotions. I know it sounds silly, but I can be at home watching a talk show featuring a man telling a story about his son who was killed in a car accident, and the next thing you know I have tears running down my face. I don't feel just a little emotion; I feel strong emotion and a real connection to the person telling the story, much more than the average person sitting on their couch eating potato chips would. This is just who I am. Long ago I realized that my emotions are finely tuned instruments that can tap into and synchronize with others. I can feel what other people feel at the same intensity and at the same time, especially sadness and happiness.

Emotion is a very important word to me. Being an empath is what helped me cross over into paranormal investigation. My hypersensitivity is a valuable skill during an investigation because spirits run the gamut of emotions, from anger to pain to sadness and confusion. This is why I took so much criticism in the early days of *Ghost Adventures*. I get it even now sometimes, like when I was emotional at Preston Castle or laughing uncontrollably at the Stanley Hotel or feeling enraged at Poveglia, Italy. I do what an empath does, and this is why my body is an important instrument during an investigation. I can sense when spirits are around me, and I can feel their emotions and energy. Sometimes it is draining and takes its toll, but it's opened me up personally. I get deeper connections and better evidence—voices, communication, orbs—because I can connect with the spirits.

How is an empath different from a psychic medium? A true medium has the ability to communicate with, and sometimes see, the dead through his or her mind. The medium makes a physical and literal connection that ends up in words being spoken though the medium. I can't do this. I just feel the spirits' emotions and try to connect that way.

There are times when I don't want to be an empath, but shutting it off is hard to do. There are times when it's embarrassing because the stereotype of an empath is a weak, sensitive person, and that's not me. There are things I'll fight for and issues I'll stand my ground on. So when I'm around a group of people and I get a sudden surge of sadness from a spirit and feel like crying, I have to fight it off. It's not easy, and it takes training. Lots of it.

The GAC gets criticized and even ridiculed sometimes because people don't realize what we're going through and can't see any paranormal activity, even though we clearly feel it. Just because there's no video or audio evidence of a spirit in a room doesn't mean that we're alone. Nick and Aaron are both sensitives. We can feel things that technology doesn't always capture. Our bodies are in tune with the paranormal; I firmly believe that. Some people say that our minds are playing tricks on us, but after hundreds of investigations, I know what I feel and what I don't. I don't expect anyone

to understand it because we live in a "show me" society, but to me it's undeniable.

We may act goofy or strange sometimes, which the haters love. "Oh, there they go...possessed again," they say, without realizing that spirits can use their energy to manipulate empaths and sensitives in a way that regular people are immune to, even though it's right there in front of them. We stay as far away from the drama and crap talking as possible because we know that we're different, and we know when we're in contact with spirits, whether they appear on camera as apparitions or not.

In *The Matrix,* Keanu Reeves is injected with new programs, and he evolves with each new packet of knowledge. It's the same for me as an empath. At every location I'm infused with new experiences, but not from today. My experiences are the war-torn hills of Gettysburg, the tribal lands of the Chumash Indians, and the hysteria surrounding nineteenth-century Salem. This makes me more well-rounded and trains me to deal with certain situations both in the real world and during investigations.

People cast on other TV shows who have no abilities but think they're experts on the paranormal disgust me. They appear on a show and suddenly they're on the paranormal lecture circuit, making mileage out of being on TV. In truth, they have no abilities and no business claiming they do. They're just regular people who can't catch any paranormal evidence, and then they tell people that their houses aren't haunted. I don't believe in that.

I BELIEVE THERE ARE A FEW PEOPLE IN THIS WORLD WHO HAVE THE ABILITY TO MAKE DEEPER CONNECTIONS WITH THE DEAD, AND I'M FORTUNATE TO BE ONE OF THEM.

6

HELPING PEOPLE

It's my mission.

Dark spirits can inflict pain and oppression on people, and their victims usually aren't taken seriously by anyone who wasn't there to witness the attack, leaving them confused and alone. I know. I've been there. So I listen to people when they talk about those traumatic events, and by doing so I catch things that most people won't. They say that when someone is in pain, another person's healing energy can comfort them, so I do my best to help people who have been victimized by supernatural forces.

Being an empath, I have a gift for comforting people when they need it. Whether they were attacked by a spirit, affected by the energy of a haunted location, or saddened by the loss of a family member or friend, I feel that and can connect with them. This is why I created the show *Ghost Adventures Aftershocks,* in which we invite people from past episodes to Las Vegas to update us on how they and their ghosts have fared since we paid them a visit.

I want to leave this world knowing that I inspired people and brought to light things that people don't understand about life. I'm not one of these goons with fame-injected egos who are cast on a show and work a season or two and think they know everything about ghosts. The paranormal is my life, and really listening to and helping people who have been affected by spirits is important to me.

When I interview people, I connect with them as an empath. I can feel their emotions. I can calibrate my demeanor to match whatever way they're projecting their experiences onto me. I truly believe that I do help people in these interviews when there are tears, anger, pain, and closure. That's meaningful to me. I don't look at myself as a paranormal Dr. Phil, and I don't compare myself to anyone else. I'm just me. This is my haunted life, and I have a long and comfortable relationship with the strange and weird. But I feel that in these interviews, I do help people work through their anger and pain and find closure.

There's no bigger reward in my life than hearing people tell me that I've helped them. Material possessions come and go, but people telling me that I made a difference in their lives by putting in the time to listen and talk to them, giving me hugs, and shedding tears—that's the meaning in my life. That's what keeps me going. It makes it easier to wake up in the morning and gives me a true purpose, more than being on TV. I'm a passionate person who cares about people, and I get great satisfaction from helping people who have been affected by spirits. It's a new part of me that I've discovered.

Life is all about finding yourself through experiences, and about learning more and more about who you are and what you're capable of. If you're getting older and not succeeding in anything or doing anything to make a positive impact on people, then you're not living. You're just waiting for death. Get out there and make an impact on people, whether it's by helping them directly or by doing research to make their lives better or just by inspiring them.

Do something good to be remembered for. This is more important than money.

I get letters all the time about how *Ghost Adventures* brings families together and helps people get through tough times. When we filmed at Brookdale Lodge in northern California, for example, one particular lady stood out to me. When we first met her, I could tell that she was traumatized by something. Part of being a good interviewer is figuring out whether people are trying to play the role of the victim in order to get attention or sympathy. Maybe they're lonely or looking for fame. There are all kinds of people out there, so I never assume that anything anyone says is true or untrue, or that a person is evil or good or whatever. But as a sensitive, I can read body language. Eye contact, tone of voice, tears…people have a lot of tells. (In another life I'd be a damn good lawyer.)

Her name was Denise, and I knew right away that she wasn't faking anything. The evidence we gathered at Brookdale indicated that there was a negative spirit there, so I believed her when she said that she'd been hurt. She began to cry when she recalled the attack during our interview, and it reminded me of my own first encounter with dark energy. When I see someone in pain from an event like this, I put my arm around them and try to transfer healing energy onto them. I'm not saying that I have healing powers through touch, but it has worked in the past, so I let my body and actions speak for themselves.

What was interesting about Denise was that soon after she left Brookdale Lodge (after being attacked many times), she felt the way most people do after being victimized by an evil spirit: She wanted to go back and confront it. Being affected by an evil spirit is not like being verbally assaulted with nasty insults or physically assaulted with a punch. The spirit injects itself into you, and a part of it stays with you. That part makes you want to return to the place where it infected you. That's the spirit's "nest," where its bad energy lives. Even though you're terrified to go back, the spirit drives you to return so that it can feed off of you like any other parasite. What I told Denise (and what I tell everyone else who has this type of encounter) is that no matter how weak you think you are, you have to be strong, show courage, and stand up to the spirit like you would to any bully. Then it won't be able to beat you. I could see the pain in her eyes and sense that something powerful and evil had affected her—yet she wanted to look it in the eye and let it know that she was stronger than it was. I really respect that.

We started filming *Ghost Adventures Aftershocks* in early 2014. It was supposed to be the paranormal version of a talk show, but it ended up changing me in so many ways. When you're trying to understand something in the paranormal field, there's nothing more powerful than sitting down and talking with people who have been deeply affected by ghosts, spirits, and demons. They're frequently traumatized and always emotional about their experiences, and for an empath like me, it can be overwhelming.

I created *Aftershocks* to show that I care about people who are affected by evil forces. I'm proud to sit and talk with those people outside the show, not for money or fame but because it allows me to help them and gives my life meaning. People who have known me for a while say that they've seen me change over the years. I've gotten older, but more importantly wiser, because I've seen the reality of the unreal. I've seen the spirit world come to life countless times, and it has affected me in a way that drives me to listen to and help people more.

Van Helsing traveled the world as a vampire slayer, and though I don't want to compare myself to any fictional figure, what I used to think was crazy has become my reality and my mission as I embark on my own travels. Discovering parts of myself that I never knew existed and identifying people who have been affected by unwelcome spirits seems to be my calling, but it's not without its drawbacks. It's hard for me to have relationships because I feel that my purpose isn't to have a traditional life, but to dedicate myself to helping people and spirits while I'm here.

Aftershocks has enabled me to find parts of Zak that weren't there ten years ago. I'm so passionate about this that I don't even call it work. Work is usually a place people go to do what they have to do, not what they want to do. Work is there for most people to make money and get by. I'm very fortunate that I get to do what I love and get by financially at the same time.

There's a special moment that occurs when I interview someone and we have a breakthrough. During every interview I can feel the person heal. There are no filters, no lying, no deception, and no worry about how the story is going to be perceived. It's all about honesty and trust. These interactions have taught me how empathetic I am toward people. I've found so many of the answers I'm looking for as a paranormal investigator not from spirits or ghosts, but from the people who have been affected by them.

Before *Aftershocks,* I'd never been so exposed to so many supercharged, powerful emotions from strangers. To see them let everything out that they'd kept inside for so long on this show and in front of me is truly humbling. It gives this show a bigger purpose than entertainment: It provides closure for these people. Communication is a powerful thing. It's how we understand each other and connect to the world around us.

The stories from *Aftershocks* are unlike anything I've heard on *Ghost Adventures.* I wasn't expecting this show to be as impactful as it is, and I wasn't expecting to be so deeply in tune with these people. When they start talking and opening up, I'm blown away. I lose track of time because I get so involved in their stories. I firmly believe that you can help a spirit find closure and pass on to the other side, and it's the same with the people who have appeared on *Aftershocks*.

One interview that sticks with me, but not for the emotional impact of the interview, was with a psychic named Liz Nowicki. I got a lot of crap from viewers after this episode, and I want to clear the air here. Liz is the resident psychic medium of the Borden House, where Lizzie Borden was accused of murdering her mother and father with an axe (she was eventually cleared by a jury of any wrongdoing). While working in the house, Liz claims to have been sexually violated by a negative spirit, so I sat down to talk with her about her experience.

Every interviewee is prescreened, so we know exactly what they're going to talk about before they come on the show. Liz's whole reason for being there was to talk about this alleged sexual attack. A lot of people were sore with me for asking questions about the assault because Liz was clearly uncomfortable during that part of the interview, but that's why she was there in the first place.

My questions were professional, and I didn't cross any boundaries at any time. I took it at a slow pace and asked her if she wanted to stop several times, which she never did. What got to me the most about this interview was that she was just as much an antagonist as she was a victim. While I felt bad for her and the things she went through, I also disagreed with her when she accused Mr. Borden of raping Lizzie. That accusation didn't sit well with me.

After people die and pass over, I don't think it's right to accuse them of horrific criminal behavior unless there's evidence of guilt, as there was in Herb Baumeister's case. Herb was never convicted, but it's been proven that he was responsible for many of the deaths that occurred at Fox Hollow Farm. (Turn to chapter 14, "Carrying Spirits," for more on that story.) To publicly state that Lizzie's father raped his daughter without having some kind of proof just isn't right, and I said so on *Aftershocks*. Liz stated that the spirit of Lizzie's mother had given her this information. That may be true, but I don't believe evidence from a spirit is strong enough to take public. I'm not saying it didn't happen, but I think Liz should have kept that information to herself.

Aftershocks is a great way to help people get over emotional trauma caused by paranormal events, but it's not just the living who need help. The spirit of Andrew Borden can't defend itself from the accusations of the living, so I chose to. I can't defend every spirit, but I can speak out for one that I've had an encounter with. There's no evidence to suggest that Andrew ever sexually assaulted Lizzie Borden.

I love doing these interviews, but what's weird is that I've struggled with anxiety disorder my whole life and sometimes have trouble getting up in front of people or being around strangers. I never thought I'd feel so comfortable being in the middle of a slew of cameras listening to someone open up about themselves so honestly. Maybe listening to them helps me get closure as well, because I find a lot of meaning in talking to them. It's addictive. It might even be therapeutic for me, when I think about it.

I can sit with a friend and talk about sports, but my mind won't be into the conversation as much as if we were talking about the paranormal. Ghosts, spirits, demons...these are the things that get me charged up. I don't just listen, I absorb. I've gained so much knowledge doing these interviews, especially about my own abilities as an empath. To hear people say that I've helped them win their battles to understand their experiences of being victimized by unseen forces is indescribable. Helping them has given my life more purpose. The darkest time of anyone's life is knowing you have a purpose, but not knowing what that purpose is. *Ghost Adventures* brought purpose to my life, but *Aftershocks* has really enlightened me. It's very rewarding.

We can't choose our family, our era, our gender, etc. But we're given this life, and in this life we learn to live no matter what fate or our environment deals us. I grew up with very little. In the late 1990s and early 2000s, I lived in a house with no furniture. My dad used to take me to the gas station and feed me bread and cheese with mustard. I struggled to find myself and my place in this world, but I always knew that I had more to offer than working in a cubicle for some company I didn't care about. I wasn't going to be anyone's puppet or work for a pension and have some fat boss say at my funeral, "Zak worked a good 45 years for this corporation, and now Jim Bob has his job. Eat your cake."

Money isn't power; helping people is. If there really is a judgment at the end of life, I'm certain that God isn't going to care about your bank account. He's only going to care about how many of His creatures you helped. We live by money. It's the blood of society. The greed of life. The root of all evil. It's what makes the world go round today. Too many people believe that the more money you have, the more power and respect you have. Just watch the show *Shark Tank* to see how billionaires treat average people with contempt. I hate the message that show conveys: that power is what we should strive for, and that money is what defines us. We're better than that. I really want to believe that we aren't selfish, pretentious assholes. And I'll admit that some wealthy people make the world better. Steve Jobs and Bill Gates have changed all of our lives. It's undeniable. They've enabled us to do things we hadn't dreamed of, like narrating this book into an iPhone.

Being told that my work helps people is the fuel that keeps me going in my career as a paranormal investigator. I don't have to prove anything to anyone, and skeptics don't call me out anymore. I think they gave up on me when they realized that I was actually doing some good. Life is not a video game where you aim for the highest score you can get before you die.

LIFE IS ABOUT HELPING OTHERS GET THROUGH THE GAME.

Donating $10K to NSPCA.

7

It Ain't Chemo

Coming face-to-face with an uncaring killer.

There are many different kinds of death. I deal with the spirits of people who have long since departed this world, and I'm very comfortable in this field. But when you encounter people whose time to depart is near and there's nothing anyone can do about it... that's a whole different ballgame.

I have a friend named Kevin Hoyt who runs It Ain't Chemo, a nonprofit organization that provides comfort to patients who are undergoing chemotherapy, radiation therapy, or other cancer treatment. It's similar to the Make-A-Wish Foundation but has no paid employees—everything is done by volunteers. Kevin called me once to ask if I would visit a dying teen who was a fan of *Ghost Adventures*. Of course I agreed.

I met Kevin at the family's home. The boy was in a hospital bed in the middle of the living room, and the cancer was so advanced that he couldn't move or speak. It doesn't take an expert to see when a person has very little time left on this Earth, and it startled me. I'd never been done anything like this before, so I'll admit that I was uncomfortable and didn't quite know what to do with myself. I wanted to be there to put some form of joy into this kid's life, but deep down it was hard for me, because as an empath I could feel his pain. On the outside I was trying to smile and be positive, but it was tough to see a child who should have had his whole life ahead of him losing it.

I felt for the family, too. Every bit of their son's life—every birthday, every school field trip, every bike ride, every friend who came over to play—all those moments they stood by their little boy were in the past, and now they had to watch him wither and die. It was gut-wrenching. I had to stay strong and be there to help make these last memories mean something to this family that had been through so much.

I brought a flashlight that I'd used on the show and autographed it for the boy. He couldn't move, so I had to open his fingers and place it in his hand. It would be one of the last times he ever found the strength to smile. The family got emotional, and so did I, even though I didn't know him. But that's the thing: You don't have to know someone for years to give a shit about him being in pain. That's just part of being human, isn't it?

I was sad to learn that the boy passed away a few days later. I'd never seen a vibrant young life dragged down by the dogs of disease up close like that. It really taught me to appreciate everything around me. The sun hitting your face, a lungful of fresh air, the ability to walk pain-free, sharing life with your family and friends… these are things most of us take for granted, but people like this boy yearn for. A life shouldn't be spent lying in a hospital bed waiting for the icy fingers of death to drag you into the unknown. Kids are supposed to play and have fun. As I write this, I'm at a hotel, and outside my room I can hear kids playing in the pool. That's how life should be for them.

The boy's smile stays with me to this day, but it scarred me, too. So when Kevin asked me to visit another dying teen, I was apprehensive. Would I end up inviting another terminally ill kid into my life and make another meaningful connection only to have him taken away in an instant? Maybe, but what else was I going to do—pretend it doesn't happen? Wish the cancer away?

Kevin asked me to meet the 15-year-old boy at Randy Couture's gym in Las Vegas one afternoon. When I got there, a few mixed martial arts fighters were teaching the boy to grapple and do some MMA moves. Kevin introduced me to him, and once again it didn't take an expert to see how sick he was. The cancer was doing its work, but the boy was lively and enjoying himself around all the fighters. I took off my socks and sat down on the mat next to him, and we talked about the spirit world and my life as a paranormal investigator. He asked a lot of questions, and I soon found myself in a real conversation about life and death with someone who would soon know much more about it than I do.

Suddenly he turned to me and said, "I'm learning how to fight so when I die I can beat the shit out of the demons that gave me this disease." It was one of the most powerful moments of my life. I've stood toe-to-toe with demons, but seeing a sickly teenager look death in the eye like that sucked the wind right out of me. He went back to training with the fighters while I stood there watching in stunned silence. I couldn't move, couldn't talk, couldn't do anything but admire his bravery. One of the reasons I've always loved MMA is the incredible courage it takes to get into a cage and fight. This boy's body was his cage, and he was slugging it out with cancer. That takes guts, but unfortunately that wasn't enough to beat the disease. A few weeks later he passed away, and again it hit me hard.

I believe everything happens for a reason, but I don't know how to interpret moments like these. I fear death, I really do. Maybe it's partly because of these encounters with people who are about to cross over at such a young age. We have so much to live for in this physical world that I want to stay here and enjoy it for as long as possible. And I don't mean that in a materialistic way. It's not the houses, cars, or belongings that make life wonderful; it's the forests, the canyons, the oceans, and all the nooks and crannies and mysteries in between that make it so special. I fear the thought of no longer being able to feel. Maybe that's the reason I was guided to help Kevin: to teach me how precious life is and to make me stronger.

IF THAT'S TRUE, THEN MY ARMOR IS SOLID.

LOCKDOWN DAY

What do we do?

"What do you do on lockdown day?"

I get this question all the time, so here's the deal.

Lockdown day is usually day three on location of a *Ghost Adventures* shoot. The first two days we knock out all the research, tech setup, background shots, B-roll footage, interviews, re-creations of events, and adventure sequences, where we do something risky to enhance the investigation. I like to find something that connects to the story of the location, like take a boat ride to the sites of shipwrecks off the coast of Point Sur, ride along with cops to see human trafficking prevention in action, or rappel into an abandoned mineshaft (I will never do that again). It's one of the things we do to distinguish ourselves from everyone else.

The third day is lockdown day, and it's always a special day for me. I usually contact Billy and Jay (who start their day at the ass-crack of dawn) to see what's going on with the tech setup. They're responsible for setting up the nerve center and wiring the four X-cameras, and being a hands-on guy, I like to know how that process is going. Early on, I go through with them where we want

72

the cameras because camera placement is crucial to the success of the production. Like real estate, X-cameras are all about location, location, location, so I'm picky about where they are set up. I want them in reportedly haunted hotspots and at intersections where they can cover lots of ground, so we place them where they can see down long hallways, especially if the camera can shoot down another long hallway easily when turned remotely. Some of them have remote heads that can be controlled from the nerve center so that Billy and Jay can see more of the location and become a fourth and fifth set of eyes for us.

The X-cameras are awesome because they're like robotic investigators. They watch our backs and help us capture evidence (both audio and visual) that we might have missed on our own. More important, they can clue Billy and Jay in if any of us are being affected by dark forces. Billy and Jay can contact us by walkie-talkie if they notice one of us behaving strangely so that we can close in on the person being affected and help him out. For example, when we were investigating the Overland Hotel, the X-cameras helped Billy and Jay see that Nick and I both needed help. Nick was definitely under the influence of a spirit downstairs, and I was on my back in the upstairs hallway after some invisible force had run through me. Billy and Jay saw it all happen on the X-cams and got us help.

These cameras also catch anomalies that manifest near us that we can later connect to a period of our being affected. I can't tell you how many times we've caught balls of light disappearing into someone's body at the same time that person became someone else.

So the positioning of the X-cams is very important, and on lockdown day I'm making sure that they're good to go. After I get out of their hair, Billy and Jay finish setting up all the electronics, which takes about five hours. Aaron and I each spend time alone and go through our own individual routines to get ready for the investigation. As you'll read about later, a lot of weird and hazardous things happen to us during these investigations, and they don't just go away when the sun comes up. A lockdown is draining and frequently takes days to get over, so we don't take this significant event lightly. I'm a big fan of mixed martial arts, so I compare my preparation on lockdown day to that of an MMA fighter on fight day. I imagine it's like a pilot who has to land a jumbo jet on a tiny dirt strip at night. He knows how to do it, but it's nerve-wracking, and throughout the flight it's in the back of his mind that a lot of people are counting on him to put this beast safely on the ground.

Aaron has a ritual that involves shaving his head with a rusty old Ginsu knife. Okay, I made up the Ginsu part, but he does shave his head. That's really all I know about what anyone does to prepare—and all I want to know. Lockdown day is a personal thing, and we respect one another's space.

In the days leading up to an investigation, I like to put myself in the shoes of the people whose spirits I'm trying to contact. I walk where they walked, sit where they sat, and feel the objects that they held dear. I really enjoy re-creating past events, too. Reenactments enable us to tune into the energy of that era, which gives us a better connection to the spirits. People criticize us for not getting straight into the investigation and taking up part of each episode with reenacting an event from the past, but there's more to paranormal investigation than putting on the equipment, going into a building, and walking around. You have to get into the right frame of mind and *feel* the location, and reenactments help us do that.

One of the most important things I do before an investigation is listen to the music of the time. For me, music is the key to lockdown prep. I like to listen to tunes that are relevant to the culture and the location: the blues in Mississippi, Creole in New Orleans, bluegrass in Kentucky, battle hymns in Gettysburg, and Native American music on reservations (I *love* the soundtrack from *Apocalypto*). Athletes often wear headphones on the day they have to perform because it gets them in the right frame of mind, and I'm no different. Anyone knowingly walking into an event where he has to be at peak performance wants to shut out the world and focus on the task at hand, and music really helps him do that. I take it one step further by using music to better understand the time, place, and people I'm trying to connect with, and maybe even bring us closer together before a lockdown, instead of just walking through the house and calling out their names. I believe that music is embedded with emotion, and if I can get myself on the same emotional level as the spirits, then we can make a deeper connection. I guess I use it both as entertainment and as part of the job, but I owe it to everyone to make every effort, no matter how small, to build that bridge between myself and the spirits.

I've always loved music because it's so powerful. Whether it's from the past or the present, music has the power to unify and comfort us. It can connect hundreds or thousands of people in an instant, whether they're sad or swaying or dancing all at the same time. We can lose ourselves in it because it enables us to exhale all the stress from our lives. Like cleansing your palate after you eat something that tastes bad, listening to music on lockdown day helps me flush 2014. It helps me clear my head of all the texts, calls, and emails I have to return, all the bad news on TV, and all the social media mentions that flood my feed.

Besides listening to music, I take time to meditate and organize myself to baseline my blood pressure and my thought process. There's a little more to it than that, but I can't give away all my secrets.

What's weird about lockdown day is the drive to the location. When it's time to meet up—call time is usually 7pm—we ride

Getting into the zone.

together, but the atmosphere is different. The goofy times are over. The setup is complete. The interviews are done. It's time to get dirty and do what we do best. We feel like a SWAT team in a van driving into a serious situation. It's a little tense because we all know it could be a dangerous night, and our only protection is our spiritual armor. We aren't really open with each other about how we protect ourselves individually. It's interesting that we keep quiet about it, actually, but it's a personal thing—prayers, cleansing, whatever processes we have we keep to ourselves.

After filming more than 150 shows and completing hundreds of investigations, I know how serious an investigation can be, what dangers we expose ourselves to, and what we can bring home to our families. We've dealt with possession, oppression, attacks, and all kinds of emotional swings, from extreme sadness to massive joy. We've all cried at one time or another, and we've even refused to continue an investigation because of how badly we were being affected. We never know what we're in for, but one thing's for sure: We can't go into *any* location unprepared.

Depending on how far away the lockdown is, I also use the drive time to prepare technically. It's probably a little bit of a defense mechanism to keep myself from thinking about the dark forces I might come in contact with, but it's my nature to check and double-check everything. So many things can go wrong, and as the lead investigator, I have to guide the team and make sure we deliver a meaningful and complete investigation and a professional product. There's a lot of pressure to deliver. It's stressful, but I'm always up to the challenge. So the drive to the location is hectic in my mind as I go through all the things that need to happen. Nothing is going to fall apart on my watch.

If someone is having a bad day, it sometimes comes out on the way to the site. Just before the Houghton Mansion lockdown, Nick and I nearly got into a fistfight over something so insignificant I can't even remember what it was now. When you're around the same people for so long, these things happen, but like any group of people who are tested and come out on top, we've evolved into a brotherhood. In the end, I have their backs and they have mine, even if we have a few dust-ups from time to time.

When we get to the location, I usually make sure that the production staff has blacked out all the windows, shut off all the lights, and cleared the area. Then I check with security to make sure that there haven't been any violations of the property. Some locations are still open to the public before we begin the lockdown, like the restaurant in the Lemp Mansion or the *Queen Mary,* so we have to take measures to make sure that people don't taint our evidence. At Union Station in Kansas City, the crew was supposed to get everyone out before we started, but for some reason that didn't happen, and our investigation of the main level was contaminated. We thought we had captured an apparition, but it turned out to be a real person who hadn't left the building yet. I was pissed, but it happens, and there's nothing you can do but move on...after uttering a few four-letter words.

Once in a while it all goes completely wrong, and we have to place the blame where it belongs: on the shoulders of the location managers. If they don't clear the place out, then we have to come right out and say that a piece of evidence isn't paranormal and the location isn't haunted after all. A successful production almost always starts with a good contact person who's willing to help. I love it when we have location managers who are grateful for us to be there; they always make the experience so much better. When they don't give a damn, everything turns out bad. We try not to make it known on camera, but it's not always Disneyland.

My last stop before a lockdown is usually the nerve center, where I make sure that the equipment checks have been done so that no technical problems arise. I hate to say it, but friendships get put aside at this point. It's all business from here on out. When the investigation starts, I'll be demanding and controlling, and the guys know it. Being responsible for the show means that sometimes I have to be an asshole. This operation ultimately falls on my shoulders and no one else's, so I can't be weak or have low standards.

In the end, lockdown day is like a perfectly choreographed circus of logistics, technology, and people. The smallest mouse being out of sync will cause a chain reaction until the elephants bring down the big top. The credibility of the Travel Channel and the reputation of *Ghost Adventures,* which we take very seriously, are constantly at stake, so it takes a lot more work than you might think to bring you an entertaining episode and a meaningful investigation.

I SINCERELY HOPE WE HAVE DONE THAT
AND WILL CONTINUE TO DO SO
EACH AND EVERY TIME.

9
RENO CRACKHEADS

A walk in the park goes bad.

Lockdown day is supposed to be my day to get right with the world, but the world has no obligation to cooperate, and sometimes things go very wrong. Now that you know what we do on lockdown day, let me tell you a story of one that got a little out of control.

We were filming at the Mustang Ranch outside of Reno, Nevada. I had a few hours to kill before heading over to the site, so I took some time to get away from everyone and relax. We were staying at a hotel in downtown Reno—a casino, I think. I didn't venture out much because I'm honestly not a big fan of Reno. I love Lake Tahoe and Virginia City, but Reno has really gone downhill. My experiences there have not been good, and this trip didn't boost its standing on the best-places-to-visit list.

The hotel was close to the Truckee River, which runs through the center of town, so I finished a workout, strapped on my headphones, and went for a walk. Everything was peaceful, and I even posted on Vine how good I was feeling when fate slapped me in the face.

I was walking along an elevated sidewalk near a wooded area when three people—a woman, a medium-sized guy, and a very dirty Andre the Freaking Giant—stumbled out of the woods. I knew immediately that something wasn't right. Their mannerisms were off, their eyes were bugged out, and they looked all around in paranoid fashion. They spoke in gibberish and had trouble walking in a straight line, so I kept my eye on them. I'm always wary of unpredictable people. We all joke about people who act weird in public and say things like, "That dude is on drugs," but these three were poster children for public intoxication.

But I laughed a little, too. I thought to myself, *Check it out... crackheads coming out of the woods, ha ha.* The joke faded when Andre the Giant started toward me and said, "What the fuck's up with you? You got a fucking problem?"

And all I wanted to do was take a walk.

I took my headphones out and he repeated himself. "I said, what the fuck is wrong with you? You got a fucking problem, dude?"

Everyone faces a confrontation at some point in life and is forced to make a decision. In a split second, you have to weigh the risks and rewards of each course of action and choose one. Swing fists? Tackle him? Tickle him? Call the cops? Walk away? Run away? Confuse him with logic? So many options, but in the end there are really only two: fight or flight. You either stand your ground and fight or turn and walk away.

To me, a street fight depends on a lot of variables. You can't just say that you'll never back down or walk away. Every situation is different. This guy clearly wanted to throw soup bones, and even though his two friends were urging him to move along, I was inclined to oblige. I don't take lightly to people messing with me or starting a fight for no reason, and I'm a little hotheaded. Maybe I should have walked away, but the part of me that hates bullies reacted, and since I had just finished a workout, my testosterone was through the roof. So, looking back on it, there probably was no decision to be made. I was committed from the start.

"What's *your* problem?" I put my arms out and returned his question. Here I was trying to relax before an investigation, thinking I was going to catch a quiet walk through Reno and listen to some Sade and make some Mother Nature Vine videos of baby ducks, and the next thing you know I'm being challenged by some whacked-out fucktard. This guy had ruined my peaceful moment, so I wasn't about to let him off the hook so easily. I walked toward them slowly, and he continued to jaw-jack while his friends tried to convince him to move on. But he wasn't having it.

"You don't want any part of this, dude," the gal said. "Walk away."

"I'm on a public street," I replied, with my fists ready. As I got closer, the giant looked more like the lovable monster from *The Goonies,* but there was nothing cuddly about him. I was thinking one punch KO at this point.

I just can't live with myself when I leave a situation and feel like I got bitched or bullied. I learned long ago that nothing scares a man more than another man who stands his ground when he shouldn't, so I stayed firm and walked toward them, while the girl kept telling me that I wanted no part of this. I honestly don't know why I kept approaching them after they'd clearly made the decision to walk away, but I did. Maybe I was just angry—angry that someone had spoiled my peaceful moment, angry at being disrespected, and angry that younger people were being dicks to their elder. The day I first stood up for myself flashed back in my mind. I wanted them to know that they had made a mistake, and maybe they'd learn something from it. Or maybe it was just about me. I'm not sure.

They walked briskly to an intersection, with the girl pushing the big guy on and the other man remaining quiet. The light turned green, and they hustled through it to create distance between us. I spotted a pair of bike cops and changed tack. Maybe a fight on a busy street wasn't the best course of action after all, and Johnny Law could remedy the situation. But when I told them I hadn't been assaulted, they took off like they didn't care. In retrospect, they didn't have any reason to arrest these jackholes other than my accusation that they were high. In my mind, this was probable cause, but what did I know?

I was disappointed, but Reno is like this. Everywhere we went that week was rough, dirty, and full of shady characters, which is unfortunate. I used to go to Reno in the early '90s when my parents lived in Tahoe, and it wasn't like that back then. It's amazing how quickly a place can change for the worse.

"So what's the point, Zak?" you're probably thinking. "You nearly got into a fight, but in the end nothing happened." Well, I left the crackhead encounter feeling like I had done some good by standing up for myself, and I wanted to pass this story on so that other people will, too. Maybe I scared them a little, and the next time they'll think twice about starting a fight for no reason, and the butterfly effect will save someone from having the same experience down the road. Or maybe I'm fooling myself, and this moment meant nothing.

We were leaving Reno the next day, but I had some time to kill after the lockdown, so I went back to the same area to look for them. I wanted closure, but I had a different goal than the day before. I didn't want to beat up the big dude as much as I wanted to confront him and make him realize the error of his ways. He clearly needed help, and the best therapy for some people is guilt. If that didn't work, then maybe he needed medical attention for whatever his addiction was. Reno used to be a great place to me, and I wanted to do something to bring it back to how I remembered it, even if it was a small gesture.

Later, I asked myself if it really would have been a good thing to get into a fight with three crackheads. Nope. I should have let them be and walked away. As we get older and wiser, we can see that the hotheaded decisions we made as youths are rarely the right ones. What do I care about a low-life druggie talking shit? He hasn't achieved one-tenth of what I have and never will, so why get into an altercation with him? Why risk everything I've built over being disrespected by someone who doesn't matter? These are the things you think of in your thirties but not in your twenties. Age has changed me for the better, I think.

But the fight didn't happen. They weren't there. They're probably still wandering around the city doing drugs and terrorizing other people.

MAYBE I'LL JUST TAKE IT AS A SIGN TO STAY AWAY FROM RENO.

10

HEALTH RISKS

This job is riskier than you think.

This life is not without risks, but the beauty of it is that we have a choice whether to take those risks or not. You can encapsulate yourself in fifty layers of Kevlar shielding, or you can be a buffalo-riding cliff diver. It's your choice. I've made a conscious decision to make connections with spirits and battle dark entities. Each time I do it, I come one step closer to unlocking the mysteries of the afterlife, but there's always a price to pay.

People don't fully understand the physical, mental, and spiritual dangers of paranormal investigation. Just as coalminers can develop black lung, paranormal investigators face undefined and possibly deadly risks. If you don't think that's true, take a walk with me through some of the hazards of my profession and then tell me if it's really something you would want to pursue.

Let's start with the physical risks. I've always had a deviated septum (see chapter 19, "Overland Hotel," for more on that), but I never had asthma until recently. I didn't have to use an inhaler until the thirtieth or fortieth investigation into a dank, moldy, asbestos- and vermin-infested hole. In the early years, I didn't

Just another day at the office.

wear a respirator during investigations. My philosophy back then was, "How can someone host a TV show with a muzzle on his face that makes it hard to hear him?" That thinking was shortsighted, and now I regret it.

Once we were investigating the Remington Arms factory in Connecticut and went underground to check out a firing range located deep beneath the facility. Aaron wasn't on camera at the time, so this isn't something you will see in the episode, but he was wearing a respirator while Nick and I weren't. It was blacker than black down there, and we were blinder than bats but without their radar. We had night vision equipment, but it sees only so much. Night vision is rarely as good as the naked eye (though it's much better in a few situations).

We were wading through an old tunnel with six inches of stagnant, muddy water soaking our feet and ankles. A hundred yards in, Nick and I started coughing—and not just a little, but a lot. It was strange, so we were forced to turn on the white lights. As soon as we did, it looked like we were in a blizzard. There were nasty particles filling the air. I don't know whether they were toxic or not, but I didn't care. We raced out of that tunnel as fast as we could, and I'm convinced that place had something to do with the breathing issues I have today.

Should we have done more research before going down there? Possibly, but so many of the buildings we go into are old and abandoned or have no existing records or custodians. They haven't been inspected or up to any kind of building code in decades, and they've got mold, lead, carbon monoxide, asbestos, chemicals, funk, crud, vagrants, hypodermic needles, and dead rodents. And it never ends. Nearly every site we investigate is abandoned.

Sometimes I worry about the breathing problems I've developed. I've been to pulmonologists, gotten X-rays, use an inhaler twice a day, and wear a respirator wherever there's a risk, but it's too late. I have issues now and will have to live with them forever.

We face other physical risks in these dilapidated rust buckets, like breaking through a floorboard, getting snagged on a rusty nail, falling down a mineshaft, running into an iron bar in the dark (Aaron is the clumsiest man in the world when it comes to such things), or having a wall fall on us. It makes me want to buy more health insurance, but try explaining what you do to an insurance representative over the phone.

Always wear protection, kids.

"You do what? And you go into these places on purpose?"

Click.

In addition to the physical dangers, the spirits themselves can harm us through attacks and possessions. I've been infested by demons, been scratched by dark entities, and had bricks and rocks tossed at me. At Pennhurst State I was nearly impaled by a coat rack with a rusty tip that I believe was thrust at me by a spirit trying to stop us from investigating. At this same location, Nick was pushed onto a pile of glass shards and received several cuts. It's no cushy desk job in a cubicle with a padded chair and a laptop. We risk our lives for this passion, and I have dozens of stories like this. I advise all paranormal investigators to take precautions. You don't want to become a ghost while pursuing them.

Spirits can be mean, too. They will try to scare you to your very core so that you'll never be the same again. We place ourselves in some of the most haunted places in the world, where people from all walks of life have experienced life-changing events and have been scarred permanently. Many of the guides we've had over the years refuse to enter the places we lock ourselves into because they've been damaged to their very souls there. They're like, "Have fun, guys. Later!"

Unless you're heartless, this job can also affect your view of humanity. We've investigated a lot of hospitals and battlefields where unimaginable atrocities took place. What some people are willing to do to others—especially those who are supposed to be under their care—is horrific and shameful. I mentioned Pennhurst State earlier, which was pure hell for the patients who suffered there, as were so many of the other sites we've visited, like Poveglia Island, the Trans-Allegheny Lunatic Asylum, Letchworth Village, Ashmore Estates, and Linda Vista Hospital. And so were the battlefields that were soaked with blood, like

Gettysburg. The hell of what people went through in these places is not easily forgotten.

And then there's the personal evolution that this job causes. Paranormal investigation is addicting, but first let's take a detour. Think about all the places you've been that may be haunted without you ever knowing it. You're walking down a hallway and have an encounter, a brief moment when a spirit interacts with you. To you it's nothing—a few goosebumps, a shudder, a quickening of your step to get away from it, and you feel normal again. But then you feel different. You're overcome by sadness or anger for no apparent reason. An inexplicable change comes over you, and you want to do something you normally wouldn't. You don't understand it and probably don't want to, but you've been bitten by a bug that injects the toxin of dark angst into you. It's rarely good. In these moments, I believe you're coming in contact with a powerful spirit that's trying to get inside you for some reason—to communicate, to educate, to harm. Maybe it needs help. Whatever its motivation, it wants to have an effect on you.

Now imagine you're me. I've overdosed on this type of encounter—I open myself up more and more to spiritual energy and other phenomena and invite them in to do what they please. It can be difficult to tell good spirits from bad ones, but coming into contact with a spirit is always a rush, and it always invites you to keep digging for more. When you become addicted—to drugs, alcohol, sugar, anything—your body deteriorates, and you begin to surrender yourself. I've started down this path, but stopped myself from continuing when I saw the signs. I've become more religious because I've seen the forces of good and evil at work, so being a paranormal investigator has given me a sense of clarity in that department.

At the Winchester Mystery House, we conducted a big experiment, attempting to make contact with dark spirits in two different locations at the same time. It's a long story, but we tried to set up a portal for demons at Bobby Mackey's Music World in Kentucky and spirits in the Winchester House in California to connect, and strange things happened to people at both locations simultaneously. At the Winchester House, Aaron collapsed in tears, and what happened to him had to be edited out because it was so personal. Something dark came through at both locations, so we cut off the experiment. But we went back into the Winchester House to continue our investigation, even though we were shaken up.

While I was walking around the hallways with a MEL meter, something terrifying happened. The MEL meter alarm went off, and at the same time my heart began beating irregularly. But here's the weird part: The meter alarmed at the exact same tempo as my heartbeat. Whatever it was detecting was moving or existing at the same pace as my heart. I froze, unable to speak and terrified that I was going to have a heart attack, so I did something I'd never done before: I cut off the investigation. I wasn't myself, and I ended a lockdown early for the first time ever. It wasn't just that I felt weird; something much deeper was wrong. Something serious and powerful told me to stop, and for once I listened.

The next day, I found out what really happened. At the exact moment my heart raced and the MEL meter alarmed, my grandmother died. That really hit me hard. I was closer to her than anyone else on my father's side of the family, and she never missed an episode. When she died, a part of me died, too. I can't believe that this is a coincidence; it's just too impactful and personal. And I don't think the electrical system in my body has been the same since then. I feel a deeper connection to spirits now.

So are the health risks of paranormal investigation real? Hell, yes, they're real. And just as risky as the physical and mental aspects is the possibility of being infested, oppressed, or possessed by dark energy. As I describe in my first book, *Dark World,* there are three levels of demonic interaction with humans:

- Infestation is the lowest level. It occurs when a demonic entity has made a nest in a building but has not yet chosen a human body to reside in. Sometimes the demon intends to remain there without disturbing the humans it comes across, and sometimes its intentions are much more dastardly.

- Oppression is the middle level. This occurs when a demon has chosen a human host and is trying to destroy that person's intellect and will. This is sometimes referred to as a transient stage, when the demon is not fully in control of the human but is trying to achieve full control. To banish a demon at this level, a priest like Bishop James Long can perform a minor rite of exorcism.

- Full possession is the highest level. At this point, the demonic entity has full control of the human host, and banishing it requires a solemn rite of exorcism. A demon can and will kill its human host if it is not banished.

At all three levels, the dark spirit manipulates the person like a leech that can't be removed. It transfuses the person with all of its dark energy, all of its pain, violence, and hate. It wants to make the person depressed and violent and cause him to turn on his family and friends.

In the early days of the GAC, we weren't aware of this risk. I first realized that oppression could happen when I saw Aaron get controlled and turn into someone else almost overnight. Before Aaron's experience, we were just inquisitive minds trying to peek behind the curtain into the supernatural world. Suddenly we knew what was back there, and everything was different. Aaron fell into a dark attachment and slowly slipped away. Out of respect for him, I won't divulge too much of what happened, but I know that this situation was caused by our insistence on pursuing the truth. We ran smack-dab into our first demon, and it wasn't a fun time.

When you investigate places where demonic attacks and attachments have been reported by significant numbers of credible sources, you are susceptible to bringing something home with you. When a spirit attaches itself to you, you become a different person but don't realize it. Only the people close to you can see the changes. The attachment can cause you to spiral into depression, detach from friends and family, and even feel suicidal. That's what oppression is: The spirit feeds on the pain it causes you to experience. You have to learn how to detoxify yourself from this energy the right way. I've been through it and still go through it. It never ends.

IT'S WHAT I DO FOR A LIVING, AND THE RISKS COME WITH THE TERRITORY.

11

HEART ATTACKS

Can spirits cause them?

I don't think people understand paranormal attacks. Hell, even I don't understand them, but I respect them, and that keeps me from getting harmed too badly. How spirits attack people is one of the things I've been researching a lot. Spirits have no mass, but they can bring a grown man to his knees. Early on, when I was a novice in this field, I would try to get attacked by calling out demons, and it happened—more often than I care to admit. And though it probably wasn't smart, it helped me learn.

Evil spirits, or the ones with bad intentions, can harm you both physically and mentally. They can scratch, burn, and bruise you or attack you with physical objects. I've seen it happen. But lately I've heard of several people having serious health issues after encounters with spirits, and even dying. Soon after completing an investigation (usually an investigation that turned nasty, where violent EVPs were documented), they fell victim to heart attacks and strokes.

At the Black Swan Inn in San Antonio, Texas, an investigator named Viktor Salazar received vulgar EVP voices saying that the spirits there wanted to kill him. Within a few months, he had a massive stroke, and his gallbladder was twisted into knots. If a spirit has the ability to manipulate you emotionally—for example, you walk into a room and feel sad or agitated—then the spirit is inside you and letting you feel its emotions. So imagine what the spirit of a violent person who enjoyed hurting people could do to you. It's definitely possible that a spirit's presence can block blood flow to the heart or brain and cause a heart attack or stroke.

In my research, I learn the most from people. I've done hundreds of interviews and investigations, and I remember every single one of them, even years later. When I hear a story from one person that's similar to a story from another person, I can connect them and see patterns. So when I found out that Viktor had caught a voice at the Black Swan Inn saying it wanted to kill him and then had a stroke (which is downright chilling), I connected it to a man named Greg Myers who had a similar experience at the Exorcist House. We interviewed Greg in St. Louis, and he told us that while he was in the bedroom where the exorcism took place, he was attacked, which was documented by a credible paranormal group. He said that the left side of his face was burned and a white cross of blisters formed on the left side of his neck. A few months after he told us this story, he had a massive stroke that affected the left side of his body.

What's interesting is that Greg felt the attack the moment it happened and had a stroke later. We used Greg's name over and over while doing our investigation at the Exorcist House, and the spirits responded. We took the Ouija board that he kept under his bed, put a spirit box on top of it, and caught voices saying, "trouble," "Ouija board," "devil," "Diablo," and "he needs help." Could the spirits actually have caused his stroke?

When he had his encounter, Greg Myers was using a Paranormal Puck designed by electrical engineer Bill Chappell. It's basically a database of words that spirits can choose by using their energy. During Greg's investigation, the Paranormal Puck said "burn" just before Greg started to feel the burning on his face. And then it said, "Paranormal investigator die." This is truly scary, because a paranormal investigator did indeed die there later. Likewise, at the Black Swan Inn Viktor caught a voice through a digital recorder that said "die," and he suffered a massive stroke afterward. It's very odd that these people documented similar evidence telling them that they were going to die and then had strokes.

In the summer of 2014, I was filming an episode of *Aftershocks* that highlighted the Mansfield Reformatory episode, and I was scheduled to interview DJ Fly, an outspoken ex-inmate of the prison. DJ Fly was haunted by the memory of another prisoner named Lockhart, who lived in the cell next to him and committed suicide by setting himself on fire. Fly nearly died in the fire as well, and the event has stuck with him his whole life (he's now in his sixties).

We were at the studio the day before DJ Fly was scheduled to fly to Vegas for the interview when we got a call from his family. On his way to the airport, DJ Fly had suffered a heart attack. His family said he had felt the pain coming on and started screaming "Lockhart," as if the spirit of Lockhart was attacking him. DJ Fly survived, and later I sent a camera crew to interview him. He said he believed that Lockhart was trying to kill him, as if Lockhart was trying to prevent Fly from coming to speak with me.

Recently, an exorcist, Father Andrew Calder, died from a stroke. He faced a lot of demons and fought them toe-to-toe over the years, and when I looked into his case it sounded similar to the other ones I've described. There seems to be a pattern to all of them. They all point to a connection between drained power sources, threats, attacks, strokes, heart attacks, and even death.

Think about this: If demons and negative spirits have the power to drain batteries, make large electronic devices malfunction by short-circuiting electrical currents, and interfere with carefully engineered electronics, then imagine what they can do to the electrical impulses within your body. And yes, we all have electrical impulses within us. Disrupting those electrical messages can lead to heart attacks and strokes.

Here's a great explanation of the body's electrical system:

"Have you ever wondered what makes your heart beat? How does it do it automatically, every second of every minute of every hour of every day? The answer lies in a special group of cells that have the ability to generate electrical activity on their own. These cells separate charged particles. Then they spontaneously leak certain charged particles into the cells. This produces electrical impulses in the pacemaker cells which spread over the heart, causing it to contract."*

Most strokes are caused by some form of arterial blockage, but some (simple strokes or cerebral hypoperfusion) are caused by a lack or disruption of blood flow to the brain, usually due to cardiac arrest. So there's a cause-and-effect at work here that we can call the Demon Stroke Theory:

1. Demons interfere with the electrical impulses of the heart.
2. The heart goes into cardiac arrest.
3. The cardiac arrest causes a stroke.

Sure, it's a theory, but we have to start somewhere if we want to fight this evil, and to me that's worth all the risks even if scientists and skeptics disagree. My most valuable research in this field doesn't come from spending time with scientists or being in

* health.howstuffworks.com/human-body/systems/circulatory/heart4.htm

a lab; it comes from spending hour after hour after hour around spirits. Scientists don't believe in the paranormal because they can't explain it (and don't want to). They have to observe everything or it doesn't exist to them. Observation is a critical part of the scientific method, which is why evolution is and always will be a theory, because no one was there to observe it over millions of years (despite mountains of evidence virtually proving that it happened).

Skeptics always say, "Science can't explain it." It's their mantra. But science can't explain a lot of things. Until a few years ago, it was believed that there were no Earth-like planets in our galaxy that could sustain life, but now we're finding them by the dozens every week. There are things we just can't control or even understand yet, and the spirit world is at the top of that list.

I've done investigations where I was able to get paranormal activity on cue, but that doesn't mean I can go to a lab and bring ghosts with me so that scientists can study them at their leisure in their own controlled environment. So even though I've experienced hundreds of paranormal events using the same equipment scientists use, paranormal investigators will always be second fiddle to them. I believe that I'm truly defying most skeptical scientists with my findings, such as the unusual evidence we collected at the Stanley Hotel with Bill Chappell.

We have to understand that we're dealing with the unexplained. We only know what we can see, hear, smell, taste, and feel; everything else is just a theory. Sometimes I feel that we humans have the mentality of a two-year-old. Why does it do that? Why is this the way it is? Why, why, why, why? We're curious beings who are programmed to ask questions, but if there isn't an answer, then it must not exist, and we ridicule it or make fun of those who do believe in it. Anyone who has spent a day in the paranormal field has experienced this kind of skepticism. "Ghosts aren't real, and you're an idiot if you think they are," people say.

But when you've been through it and start to make these connections, you really start believing that you're on to something. And sometimes I wonder if I'm getting myself into trouble by starting to figure it out—like the spirits know I'm beginning to understand their world and aren't happy about it. I've had friends in this field who have literally gone crazy, and it makes me wonder if they were getting too close to the answers that powerful forces didn't want them to know. But we'll never know until we cross over. That's how God made it, and I do believe in Him.

IT'S ALL A DESIGN, AND IT ALL HAS MEANING...
EVEN THE HEART ATTACKS.

12

ROMANIA

A little salt goes a long way.

I hate flying like a pirate hates a toothbrush. You could accurately describe me as having pteromerhanophobia, but that's way too long a word to use casually. It's easier to say that I have acrophobia, which is a fear of heights. This is true, but being at a high altitude and hurtling through space at the same time brings on a whole new kind of fear for me. It's not so much that I don't trust the engineers who designed the plane or the pilots flying it, but I hate not being in control. If I'm driving a car and things go badly, then at least I can take control and get myself out of the situation. If something goes wrong with a plane, all you can do is tuck your head between your legs and pray. So I'd rather chew on tin foil than fly to Romania, but I did it because my desire to investigate Vlad Dracula's castle and birthplace was greater than my fear of going down like a lawn dart somewhere in the Atlantic. We all have to face our fears eventually.

About three weeks before I flew, anxiety began to build up, and the second I got onto the plane, claustrophobia punched me in the gut. I was like Ed Norton in *Fight Club*: I could envision crash after crash, and every little thing had me second-guessing my reasons for being there. This is what flying does to me: When the cabin doors lock and I know I'm going to be trapped in that aluminum tube for eons, I hit a whole new level of panic. Most people would recommend psychotropic drugs or relaxants, but I can't do that. I hate putting that stuff in my system. So I all I can really rely on is my iPod. It's saved my sanity on several occasions.

When I fly, I watch the flight attendants for clues. If they're calm, I'm good. If they're freaking out, then I will, too. Turbulence is the worst. Every little bump rattles me, and I really don't like it when the captain comes on the intercom and tells everyone to have a seat and fasten their seat belts. Then I know we're in for some shit that will take years off my life.

I flew directly from Las Vegas to France and then boarded a new plane to Romania. Even though I had a sleeping seat, I couldn't sleep. It's just not me. When we landed in Bucharest, I felt like I'd stepped out of the phone booth in *Bill & Ted's Excellent Adventure*. Everything was new, exciting, and strange. I love moments like that, but it was such a relief to be on terra firma that I couldn't enjoy it much. Being at a high level of anxiety for so long is a drain, and all I really wanted to do was get to my hotel room and decompress.

Not Aaron. He always wants to go walk around, probably because he drinks eight cups of coffee a day and has a ton of energy. Aaron always wants to do something, which I admire even if I don't want to go along. He's a thrill-seeking adventurer, and unfortunately he's good at convincing the rest of us to follow his lead. Aaron will spend no more than five minutes in his hotel room before he texts everyone to go out and look around. We call him The Walker. He'll walk for miles just to see the sights, and he never takes a cab.

Sure enough, he did exactly that in Bucharest. I should have seen it coming. After being on a plane for so long, there was no way he'd sit idle in his room, and I was too curious to fight him. After all, when would I ever be in Romania again?

So we went walking around Bucharest and quickly met up with our fixers. Fixers are production managers on location. Their job is to help us out-of-towners with everything—logistics, security, navigation, communicating in the local language, you name it. We put our lives in the fixers' hands. They could take us out into a field and kill us for all we know, but we trust them. So far we haven't found a reason not to. I've had hundreds of fixers over the years, and in Bucharest we had two: Andre and Crazy Name. Andre was awesome. He was a cool-ass dude, and I really enjoyed his company.

Andre and Crazy Name took us out, and I began to notice how many stray dogs there were. Later I learned that Romania has the highest population of stray dogs in the world. They're like birds in America. There were hundreds of dogs everywhere we went, and as a dog lover and activist against animal cruelty, I couldn't help but notice them. I fed them whenever I could, like sausages from gas stations. This was always risky because the second I broke out food, the packs would come running, and I never seemed to have enough to go around.

The next day we drove to Sighisoara to film our show where Dracula was born. Billy Tolley, Andre, and I rode together. Every mile or so along these Romanian roads, we noticed a bunch of women. I'd never seen so many women just walking along the road, so I asked Andre what was up. He told me that they were gypsies. To us Americans, the word *gypsy* conjures up all kinds of magical images, and I was intrigued to see some in person. Maybe they have some sort of genetic connection to the spirit world and could help me understand it better?

Unfortunately, in Romania, gypsies are a minority that's treated very badly. They're considered dirty, untrustworthy creatures and subhumans, which saddened me, especially when I found out why there were so many of them on the open roads. Andre told me that many of the women we saw were prostitutes selling their "goods" to passing drivers, but they also had a way of making a legitimate living. Every few miles there were tables manned by gypsy women where they sold homemade honey, sap, and CHEESE! I love cheese, so we stopped at one of these tables, and I bought five big hunks of cheese and a little bit of honey.

But I didn't really think it through. It was hot during the day, with temperatures reaching into the upper 80s, and I had no way of cutting into these cheese bricks while we were filming. So five giant blocks of cheese sat in Andre's car, getting hotter and hotter. One of the bricks that I left under my seat basically cooked and saturated

The cheese stand in Romania.

Andre's car with its funk. It was like stinky, sweaty feet that had been wearing boots for a month and then marinated in rotten egg salad. I felt awful that I had jacked up Andre's car so badly. By the end of the trip, it was rank. To this day, if Billy or I ever smell that type of cheese again, we'll puke all over the place, like the kids in *Stand by Me* did.

We filmed for a day in Sighisoara and had a great shoot. Afterward Billy and I got in Andre's stinky cheese car to drive to a town called Cluj-Napoca—in a different part of the country away from everyone else—but I quickly developed a problem. My asthma was acting up, and I didn't have a rescue inhaler with me. It wasn't bad enough that I was in danger of dying from a completely closed airway, but it was uncomfortable to say the least, and the stench of my cheese didn't help.

Keep in mind that not all of Romania has modern roads. We were driving along kidney-jarring back roads for a long, painful time...with asthma and stinky cheese funk. It may have been the worst road trip of my life, and we had a long way to go to Cluj-Napoca to film in the Hoia-Baciu Forest. Another car went with us to carry the gear, and the driver of that car (who was also a dentist) also had asthma and saw that I was in agony. At a rest stop, he told us that to cure my ails we needed to stop at a salt mine that was on the way. I've never heard of smelling salts being used as a treatment for asthma and was immediately against it. I just couldn't see how it was going to help.

But the dentist was convincing. He said that people come to these salt mines from all over the world to cure their ailments, so I reluctantly agreed, and we set off for the middle of nowhere, Romania. Remember what I said about fixers being able to take us anywhere and leave us for dead? This could have been the intro to a horror film.

We drove a long way through forests, past giant medieval castles, and through gypsy towns where huge cranes built nests under the protection of the locals. These magnificent birds looked to be five feet tall and were well cared for, because the gypsies believe that cranes who have babies bring good fortune. It's funny how some animals are considered evil and hunted, while others are considered sacred and protected. Luck of the draw, I guess.

We finally arrived at the salt mine, and let me tell you, it was a crazy place. First we boarded a shuttle bus full of people and drove into a cave in the side of a mountain. It was pitch black, and I felt like I was on Mr. Toad's Wild Ride at Disneyland. The bus narrowly missed every wall. Even stranger than the drive were the people, who looked like they were going to the gym with towels, exercise clothes, headphones, and bags full of recreational equipment. I felt so out of place, which is saying a lot for a guy like me.

The bus stopped, and everyone went through a door to come face-to-face with the staircase from hell. It was straight down and looked to be at least 500 steps. *Wait,* I thought. *I have a respiratory problem. If we go down there, how am I going to get back up?* I didn't want to go, but those jackholes talked me into it. I would have felt like a quitter if we traveled all that way and I didn't even try, so down we went. Instantly I tasted salt in the back of my throat and took some deep breaths. I wanted to scramble back up to the surface with every step, but I forced myself to tread on.

When we reached the bottom, I was dumbstruck. Through a corridor was a huge cavern, and people were enjoying themselves like beachgoers in Jamaica. There were Ping-Pong tables, shuffleboard games, restaurants, taverns, and even tents for people with more severe respiratory problems who stayed for weeks at a time. It was very weird but also very cool, and it took only a glance for me to realize that this was probably a good thing. I felt bad for doubting the fixers. They are chosen to be fixers because they have an innate knowledge of the local community and can be relied on to take care of us foreigners.

Apparently the salt mines attract people who need to breathe the negatively charged air; it brings them comfort without the use of pharmaceuticals. So we had lunch and hung around for a while. I made it back up the stairs and felt a ton better. For the rest of the shoot, I had no respiratory problems at all. It was a detour I'll never forget, and I am so glad I took it.

Until I had to get on a plane to come home.

AS GOOD AS MY LUNGS FELT, I STILL HATED FLYING.

13

NETHERWORLD

I'm an official member of the Sabretooth Vampire Clan.

Like most creative types, I have a mind that never stops working. I'm always looking for new ways to say and do things. Last year I came up with an idea for a new TV show where I would travel the world and explore various cultures and their beliefs about death and the afterlife. I wanted to take *Ghost Adventures* one step further and dive into other cultures and their taboos. Originally it was called *Dark World*, but I changed it to *Netherworld* and got the funding I needed to film a pilot episode.

The pilot was supposed to be shot in Haiti, where we would investigate real-life zombies. Haitian legend states that there's a cemetery where rituals take place that make people catatonic. The locals bury these catatonic people, but supposedly some of them rise up out of the ground still alive, like zombies. (The movie *The Rainbow and the Serpent* is based on this topic.) So I got the necessary vaccinations and prepared to fly to Port-au-Prince for a new adventure. But obstacles kept popping up that prevented us from doing the episode, so we switched to our backup plan and went to Paris to film in the catacombs instead. I was disappointed, but

The Paris catacombs.

I was confident that we could make a great show about the legendary underground cemeteries. Paris seemed tame compared to Haiti, but it ended up having a bigger impact on me than I ever expected it to.

The Paris catacombs have a long and sordid history, and there are plenty of legends and mysteries to explore in the massive maze of tunnels that lie just below the streets. They were originally limestone mines on the Left Bank of the Seine River, but in the eighteenth century the mines were converted to depositories for the bones of the dead. Millions of bodies were dumped there over decades of plagues, famines, wars, you name it. It's easy to see how stories of werewolves, ghosts, and all sorts of strange creatures spread quickly.

I took a direct flight from Las Vegas to France, which was nine or ten hours in the air. If you know anything about me, then you know I have trouble with flying. I hated being in a plane for so long, but even worse was the production schedule that was waiting for me when I landed.

I got to Paris late at night, went to the hotel, tried to sleep, and got up at around 6am to film for something like twelve or fourteen hours. When I film overseas, I like to have a day to adjust to the new time zone, shake off the jet lag, and get acclimated to the new location. My face gets puffy after being in a plane for so long, which doesn't look good on camera. It sounds superficial, but I make my living on TV, and when I have double bags under my eyes, it's noticeable. In post-production for this particular episode, we had to cut several shots because of how tired I looked. Not good.

For three solid days, I was filming every possible second and barely had time to sleep. I'm a warrior and really wanted this project to succeed, so I manned up, but to do all this for a pilot was really unnecessary. A pilot episode is like an experiment. You're not sure if the idea has legs, so you spend some time and money exploring the concept to see if it resonates with fans. If it does, then you keep going. If it doesn't, then you haven't lost much. Even though I was the executive producer and the man in charge, I was a little upset with my producers who had put together such an aggressive schedule.

As a documentary filmmaker, I have only so much material provided by the researchers and producers to work with. A list of interviews is really about it, because the filmmaker has to have the freedom to take the story where it needs to go. A documentary film isn't scripted; it's an exploration into the unknown. I'm more than just the host. I'm the lead creative executive producer and director, so I call the shots on what to shoot and how I want to feed off the interviews and develop the story. That's my right, and I take it very seriously.

The ability to do an interview with a central figure and take the story further makes the story more interesting for the viewer. I'm bloodthirsty when it comes to uncovering breaking news and finding new material to push the boundaries of the story and delve into details that weren't known before. This is how I define myself as a host, director, and filmmaker. But the tight production schedule made this very difficult in Paris, and it took everything I had to stay focused on developing the story. Some filmmakers wouldn't be able to deal with it, but I work best under pressure and have the ability to overcome obstacles and adapt, so I set out to do just that.

We were deep into the second day of filming when I was informed that no one could find Francis Friedland, the man who had discovered the missing video footage that was a centerpiece of the *Netherworld* story. His experience was critical to the story, so we hired a fixer to find him. Thank God she was so good at her job. She did what no one else could and became an absolute savior for this production. I was desperate for a break when we got the call that she'd found Friedland. I was happier than Pharrell when I got the news.

Like a journalist getting a hot tip, you have to act on a break like this. It doesn't matter if you can barely stand up (and I was exhausted at that point); a professional finds the strength to pursue the lead. I told my people to get me a car, get me to where Friedland was, and set up an interview, which we did in a café immediately after finding him. Typically only Nick and Aaron are with me when I film an interview for *Ghost Adventures,* but *Netherworld* was astronomically bigger. Seven cameras were shooting Friedland, which turned out to be a logistical nightmare but made for a powerful interview. Afterward I was very excited, and I felt that the footage added a lot of value to the show. I was truly on a mission, and that mission was captured in that interview.

At a particular point, though, the exhaustion finally caused my temper to boil over.

On the last day of filming, I was asleep in my hotel room. I had filmed all night the previous night and had hiked something like five miles through the catacombs with the cataphiles. After two full, intense days, my knees and back ached and I just wanted to sleep a little, but my producers pressed me to squeeze in more interviews, so I got up and complied. I was so tired that I had to wear sunglasses because my eyes were double-bagged. In these situations, it's a challenge to stay engaged in the interview, but you have to keep up your energy no matter what your state of mind, or you lose your enthusiasm and then lose the viewers. Stale interviews are land mines in TV. As soon as it gets boring, people change the channel, and your ratings get blown to bits.

As the camera crew was setting up for the interview in a beautiful historic plaza, I noticed a nearby concession stand that was selling Nutella crepes. I love those things. Nutella is like Axe Body Spray; chicks love the smell of it. The person who makes Nutella cologne will be a billionaire. Anyway, I ran over to the stand to grab a crepe, and Jay, one of my camera guys, followed me. As I stood in line, Jay was shooting me through the opposite window of the concession stand so he could see my face when the owner suddenly lost his temper.

Something set this guy off, because once he saw Jay, he started screaming at him to give him the camera footage and his SIM card. Then he started yelling at a female crew member who had come over to help. He tried to grab the camera from Jay's hands, and the next thing we knew, the dude held up a knife. The situation escalated quickly, and I snapped. I was tired, hungry, and generally grumpy when this guy threatened to kill a member of my crew.

Oh, hell no.

I yelled at him to come around to my side of the stand so I could beat his ass, and I had to be carried away by more crew members. I was incensed that he had threatened my people and wanted blood. We actually got the whole incident on film, but we decided not to use it because it didn't contribute to the story, and in the end Paris was good to me. I knew that this incident wasn't indicative of that great city. This is the fortunate part of working around a lot of cameras: You can record everything and use the footage to defend yourself when people make false claims about you.

After calming down a little, I went into the interview with my guest, Father Sebastiaan, who had witnessed the whole incident. I'm sure he thought I was crazy in the beginning, but we ended up having a great interview and even became friends. He was so knowledgeable about many different facets of the catacombs and the Paris subculture. By then, we already had a lot of great material, but his insight was invaluable.

One of the things Father Sebastiaan told me was the story of King Louis XVI and Marie Antoinette, who were both executed by guillotine during the French Revolution. After their execution, the people threw their bodies into the catacombs, and even though the bodies have been exhumed and moved, parts of them are still believed to be down there. It's kind of crazy to think that there could be royalty carelessly tossed in among the millions of skeletons lining the catacombs. You could be walking through the tunnels and pick up a random skull and not even know that it once belonged to a king or queen.

After the interview, Father Sebastiaan told me that he is the Master Fangsmith for the Sabretooth Vampire Clan. Yes, there really is such a group. It has several thousand members, and he's one of the head honchos. The Sabretooth Clan is one of the largest

Father Sebastiaan gives me my fangs at the White Rite.

"Zak is a natural addition to the Sabretooth Clan and Family. We are highly passionate about our own creative endeavours and highly individualistic with our own life goals and paths. What makes the Sabretooth Clan strong is this diversity of individuals inspiring each other and not competing. Zak is an inspiration for each individual to truly be who they are and find their own 'Vampire Gifts' and follow them intensely."

—*Father Sebastiaan*

in the world, so this was very cool to me, especially when he asked if I wanted to be initiated into the clan. How could I refuse?

It seemed like fate in a way. I've always been intrigued by the vampire culture, and long ago I met a group of vampires in Scotland (which I wrote about in *Dark World*). I kind of feel like I *am* a vampire—not in the way Hollywood portrays vampires, but in the way the vampire culture really is. Vampires train their souls for the afterlife and train to live as immortals after their first death. Everyone thinks vampires are the way they're portrayed in movies—they drink blood, have super powers, and are immortal. That's not the way I am. Just like there are different sects of a religion, there are different kinds of vampires. Vampirism to me is a way to prepare your soul for the afterlife and be comfortable with your own dark side. It's hard to put into words, but it's a fascination that's turned into an addiction that's turned into a reality now that I'm part of the Sabretooth Clan.

Father Sebastiaan asked me to meet him in the basement of a gothic bar so I could be initiated in the White Rite. As the Master Fangsmith, he molded and sculpted my own set of vampire fangs and welcomed me into the order. It just so happens that he's a dental technician, too, so his casts are some of the best and most authentic in the world. He's made fangs for many famous people, so he's legit. (He is also the author of *Vampire Magick* and *Vampire Virtues*, which are fascinating reads.)

When I put the fangs in my mouth, they just felt right. They made me feel different, and I embraced it. It's almost like wearing a cloak of power that protects me when I encounter evil spirits. The fangs are a symbol, like any other religious symbol that empowers your soul and represents the virtues by which you live your life.

My background in communicating and developing deeper connections with spirits was valuable to Father Sebastiaan's work. As the High Priest of the clan, he develops and preaches the gospels that guide us, and my work with the afterlife is a part of that. It helped get me inducted into the clan, and I was happy to accept this gift, no matter how tired I was after three days of intense filming.

IT MADE THE WHOLE TRIP WORTHWHILE.

14

CARRYING SPIRITS

Can a human being harbor a second spirit?

Here's a theory: We travel the world looking for ghosts and waiting for spirits to show themselves at all hours of the day and night, desperately seeking that moment when they'll make themselves clear to us. But what if they're right in front of us the whole time and we just can't see them? What if there are spirits living inside the people we encounter every day?

Typically, when heinous acts occur in a house, the location is stigmatized. (Think of the Sharon Tate murders in the mansion on Cielo Drive north of Los Angeles.) The house is demolished, the address is changed, and a new structure is built to erase the shame. But it doesn't always work, and the spirits carry on.

The second you set foot on the property at Fox Hollow Farm in Carmel, Indiana, you can feel that something very bad happened there. Our trip to the farm to film an episode of *Ghost Adventures* was weird and disturbing. The bodies of eleven men were discovered on the property in the 1990s, and the owner, Herb Baumeister, was suspected of luring them all there to kill them (and was suspected of nine more murders away from the farm). Baumeister never confessed to the murders and committed suicide before he could be convicted, so one of the worst serial killers in American history remains a mystery.

Still, it's an undeniable fact that eleven men were killed on that farm. It may seem strange, but to me it felt like every piece of that property was holding onto those grisly deaths. It was infected, as if the bodies had fertilized the ground with their anger, as if nature itself had been affected by those heinous acts.

While we were doing our research on Fox Hollow Farm, I learned the details of Herb Baumeister's suicide. He fled to Ontario, Canada, and was found dead of a gunshot to the head on a bed of sand on the shores of Lake Huron. He was found with his arms straight out and dead birds surrounding him. He killed himself in a ritualistic way, and that stuck with me.

Rob and Vicki Graves were the owners of the farm when we conducted our investigation. When I interviewed them and stared into their eyes, I could tell that something wasn't right. I felt like it wasn't them I was seeing. It was beyond them being uncomfortable; it was as if Herb's spirit was affecting them. Vicki seemed more submissive than I felt she should have been, and I'd read that Herb had the same relationship with his wife, Julie (who refused to let the police search the house for months until she was convinced that Herb was up to no good and had filed for divorce). Was he in the room, projecting himself onto the family like he had done to Julie?

This uneasy feeling combined with a strange heaviness inside the house put me in a mood. The air felt stagnant, and in nearly every room I felt like I was being watched, which affected me. I wasn't my typical loud, enthusiastic, effervescent self, and I wasn't clear. I wasn't conducting a good interview, but I felt like I had the engine of a fifty-year-old car whose oil had never been changed. I was sluggish and lethargic and couldn't figure out why. Moments like this lead me to ask: Are the people who live in places plagued by gruesome events carrying those spirits inside them?

There's a theory in the paranormal community called the Stone Tape Theory, which says that certain natural materials can act like tape recorders and store the energies of the living. According to this theory, an event, usually one that involves a great deal of emotion or trauma, can somehow be captured in the stonework surrounding it and then replay like a recording under certain conditions. For example, an apparition of a miner running down a tunnel yelling, "Cave in!" could be an event that was recorded by the rocks themselves. The energy from that event is stored and can be released at any given moment, resulting in a playback that can be both heard and seen. The spirit usually acts out the event with no regard for the living in its presence.[*]

Fox Hollow Farm has barely been renovated since the Baumeister family lived there. It has an intercom system, and each time I touched it, I had visions of Herb using it to try to hunt down his victims inside the house. In the kitchen there was a 1980s can opener that popped up out of the counter. I pushed a button and it popped up, and I imagined Herb opening a can of beans with it. The Stone Tape Theory suggests that objects like these that were present during traumatic events can hold onto those events. But can *people* harbor the spirits of those who are no longer with us?

Baumeister killed himself in a ritualistic manner for a reason. Serial killers have to have control and work off of controlling their victims. They're smart. They kill and get away with it, often for a long time. That takes meticulous planning and intelligence, and though I'm certainly not praising them, it's not for the idiots of the world.

---

[*] Zak Bagans, *Dark World*, Section VI

So how does a ritualistic suicide in Ontario matter in Indiana? The way Herb killed himself tells me a lot about how this family is still being affected by him. I think that he killed one bird for each of his victims, believing that it was a way for him to remain earthbound instead of going to hell. I think he did this because he believed that he could stay in the house and continue to control anyone who lived there. But he treats the Graves family the same way he treated his own family, with respect.

So is Herb's spirit still there, and is he possessing or controlling Rob Graves? Is Graves carrying around the spirit of Herb Baumeister unknowingly? The whole time we were searching for Herb's spirit and believing that we were coming into contact with the spirits of his victims, were we actually talking to Herb in a way? After all, the Graves family lives in the same rooms that Herb inhabited and uses the same everyday items that Herb used.

Vicki Graves said that she felt scared at times, especially in the master bathroom, and she would shake at the thought of being in the presence of Herb's spirit. Rob, however, didn't flinch. He was adamant that the spirits were there in the house because "[Herb] liked it here, and the victims are still here." He even had a creepy demeanor at the times when Vicki seemed the most scared. Sometimes as we filmed, I would catch Rob watching us through the blinds, as if through Rob, Herb was keeping an eye on us so that we didn't learn too much (or maybe to ensure that we saw something he wanted us to see). Rob also got uncomfortable when we talked about certain parts of Herb's life. I'm not saying that Rob Graves is a serial killer, but I couldn't shake the idea that the spirit of Herb Baumeister could be affecting him. I think if you spend a long time in a place filled with bad energy, that energy becomes a part of you, and that's what was happening at Fox Hollow Farm.

The people who live in the locations we film for *Ghost Adventures* often ask us to investigate over here or over there, or ask us to come in early so we can find more, without realizing that the spirits are actually the ones guiding them. The spirits know what happened there and channel that information through the living. This was true of Fox Hollow Farm. The family pointed out details of the property, and I kept wondering if it could be the spirit of Herb (or his victims) channeling information through them.

As I said earlier, many places where mass murders or other atrocities occur are changed or torn down in order to wipe away the memories. The ones that survive (like the Viscilla Axe Murder House in Iowa) are usually turned into tourist attractions. But Fox Hollow Farm was different. Not only was it still intact, but a family was living there among the remnants of Baumeister's life. They swam in the same pool in which Baumeister drowned people. They showed me pictures of bones of unnamed victims that they found popping up out of the ground in the backyard. Items that Herb might have used as murder weapons, like the hose with which he strangled some of his victims, were still being used. A serial killer is the closest thing to a demon walking the Earth, and this family was living in his house with all the same stuff. Being there was

(NOT SO) FUN FACT:

WHILE WE WERE FILMING A SOUND BYTE IN THE BACKYARD (WHERE THE BONES WERE FOUND), SOMETHING COMPELLED ME TO LOOK UP AT THE UPSTAIRS WINDOW. WHEN I DID, A CURTAIN DREW OPEN AND ROB GRAVES STARED BACK AT ME, BUT ALL I REALLY SAW WAS HERB BAUMEISTER LOOKING AT ME. SCARED THE CRAP OUT OF ME.

deeply disturbing, and I can't help but think that the Graves family was being affected by Herb's spirit.

The whole time we're looking for spirits in the nooks and crannies of a place, the spirit may actually be found in a person who lives there. Many spirits just want their physical bodies back, after all. They want to smoke a cigarette, eat a pancake, lay out by the pool, and feel the wind on their face or the touch of a loved one.

The David Oman house in California is another prime example of a person rather than the location itself being haunted. David lives in a house that even the most intelligent and respected paranormal experts fear to enter. Barry Taff is a parapsychologist and PhD who has done more than 4,500 investigations using the most advanced equipment, yet he says that the David Oman house is the only place he feared to set foot in again after investigating it once. Dr. Taff claims that the house almost killed him and that nearly every time he goes there (more than twenty visits so far), he winds up in the hospital. So I had to ask: How could someone live there and not be affected?

When I met the owner, David Oman, I knew right away that something wasn't right with him. I couldn't tell if it was personal, mental, or the house, but it didn't take long for something powerful and dark to affect me and my crew. It seemed to control David Oman and was trying to gain control of us, too. The question was, what was it? The spirits at Fox Hollow Farm were easy to identify because of the murders that had been committed there, but the David Oman house was different. As far as we knew, no deaths had occurred on the premises. The house was in close proximity to the mansion where Sharon Tate and her friends were murdered by members of the Charles Manson cult, but that was all we knew of, and those murders had occurred at least 200 yards away in a house that's no longer there. Oman was quick to tell us that he feels he's being affected by Tate's spirit, but Dr. Taff felt that something more was going on, and I agreed. Taff described the energy of the house:

> My instruments (Geomagnetometer, Natural Tri-Field Meter, Air Ion Counter, etc.) indicated bizarre and totally unprecedented magnetic field amplitudes and polarities throughout the entire house combined with an ambient electromagnetic background anywhere from 20–100 times normal. This house was a compass needle's worst nightmare. In fact, there were several locations in David's home where compass needles would spin wildly as if near a quadrapole, which does not occur in nature. And on other occasions almost everything in the house seemed to be emitting a very strong magnetic field, including glass, wood, plastic and leather. None of which are ferromagnetic or paramagnetic…
>
> While on the stairwell, disembodied voices could be heard, but [were] not always recordable. At times, it sounded like someone loudly snoring or with severe asthma. At other times, it was like very muffled conversations were occurring. If I stood on the stairway too long, I became dizzy and nauseous.[*]

Even more amazing is that the David Oman house allegedly sits on Native American burial grounds—never a good idea. Benedict Canyon is said to have been a sacred burial area for native tribes, but there's no way to know for sure whether this is true. There were no historians, no record keepers, and no technologies to record their lives. But we do know that natives lived, fought, sacrificed animals, and buried their dead in this area. They had no crystal ball; they couldn't have foreseen that one of the largest cities in the world would one day overtake their sacred land with tractors, homes, technology, parties, and even murders.

---

[*] http://barrytaff.net/2013/07/cielo-drive-convergence-the-ultimate-field-laboratory/

We have to remember the way native tribes thought. They had a relationship with Mother Nature on this land, and then we came along and desecrated it. Can you blame them for being pissed? I believe it curses the spirits and taints the energy there. The land is not supposed to be disturbed, let alone have houses built on it. It's like an Egyptian sarcophagus that shouldn't be opened. In my opinion, the Sharon Tate murders only agitated the energy even more. I think those heinous acts awakened something in the ground that either wants them to leave or wants vengeance, and whatever spirits were awakened are so strong that they are also affecting David Oman.

David is a nice guy, but we had issues with him. When the cameras were off, he liked to argue. He would be nice one minute and then be causing problems with the crew the next. He made the biggest deal of the smallest issues, like a mark on a wall that made him snap. We were wary around him and almost scared of him at times because he was so unpredictable. He could turn into someone else at the drop of a hat. But was that really him, or was something manipulating him?

David seemed to know when something paranormal was about to happen in the house. We were interviewing him once with the camera off, and he could tell us when figurines were going to fall over or loud noises were going to be heard. He seemed to have a relationship with the spirits, and Dr. Taff even said that he may be a "poltergeist host." He talked to the spirits the way a parent talks to a noisy child when the family has company: with terse scolding. At times we were almost investigating David instead of the house. Dr. Taff was definitely afraid of him.

David Oman is another example of spirits living inside or through human beings, I believe. The affected people take on bizarre personalities and unpredictable behaviors. When I look into their eyes, I don't see the person, but the spirit inside them—not their own spirit, but the spirit of someone else who's passed over. They are half alive and half dead, almost like zombies. They have a hard time answering questions because they confuse the history of their own life with the history of the spirit inside them...like half their life is gone, or they just can't remember it. Haunted locations can change people.

MAYBE THE SPIRITS WHO REFUSE TO LEAVE THAT LOCATION ALSO REFUSE TO LEAVE THE PEOPLE WHO LIVE THERE.

15

DOLLS

I hate them.

Believe it or not, this is easily the hardest chapter of this book to write, so it won't be long. I hate dolls almost as much as I hate clowns, but for a different reason. When I'm around dolls, I can feel their eyes looking at me, and even though I know they're not human eyes, it makes me very anxious, because I honestly believe that dolls can harbor spirits better than any other objects. To you, dolls may seem like harmless inanimate objects or playthings for children, but to me they're vessels for spirits, and they scare me to the bone.

I'm not alone here. Hollywood tends to depict dolls in evil, horrible forms—think Chucky, Jigsaw, Blade, and the super-nightmarish clown doll from *Poltergeist*. Of course they're not real, but I look at them a little differently because I have a theory that dolls can store paranormal energy better than most inanimate objects. There's one simple explanation for this: They've been loved.

To a child who receives a doll as a gift, the doll is alive. It's everything to them. They name it. They nurture it. They dress it up and talk to it like a friend and take it everywhere. To the child, the doll is real, just like everyone else around them. Children put a lot of love and feeling into their dolls, and I believe that some dolls not only retain that emotion, but also become doorways for spirits to get back to the physical world. And a doll can become a nest for a spirit to roost in after it's crossed over. So when I see one, I don't see factory plastic and fake horsehair; I see a container that could be holding a spirit.

This isn't an entirely new theory. Shabti dolls were ancient Egyptian figurines that accompanied the deceased to the afterlife to carry out specific duties. They've been found in tombs dating back as far as 1500 BC. Each one represented a worker to serve the dead after he left this world. Each doll was inscribed with a spell, which outlined what that worker was supposed to do when he met Osiris, the god of the dead, and was asked to carry out his duties. So it was believed that the dolls actually crossed over with the person who died.

In the present, every paranormal group I've ever seen uses dolls as trigger objects to attract child spirits. They do this because it's effective at encouraging a spirit to manifest, right? Maybe, but I think there's more to it. I don't think that using a doll brings a spirit closer; instead, the doll attracts the spirit to possess it. The doll becomes a container for the spirit to get into and manipulate, like a person opening a car door, stepping in, and taking it for a spin. Dolls are not just trigger objects to attract spirits, but can actually carry spirits and even be possessed by them...and usually not the good type.

When we filmed the Island of the Dolls episode of *Ghost Adventures,* I knew that I was in for an uncomfortable, emotional ride. On this island that lies between the canals of Xochimilco south of Mexico City, there is a swamp where a little girl drowned under strange and disputed circumstances. A man named Don Julian

Santana Barrera saw a floating doll in the canal and assumed that it belonged to the girl. He picked up the doll and hung it from a tree as a way of showing respect and supporting the spirit of the girl. But he didn't stop there. Don Julian hung thousands of dolls around the island for the little girl and believed that her spirit possessed them. After being there, I don't disagree.

A local psychic medium said that a snake-like negative spirit was the cause of the girl's drowning. So many legends surround that ancient Aztec canal that I don't doubt it. It's a very scary place to go, whether you have a fear of dolls or not. If the girl's spirit is truly trapped on that island and all these dolls attract her, then I think other spirits can also be attracted to her and the thousands of dolls as well. I believe that the spirits connect through the dolls, which basically makes this place my nightmare. Think about this: who knows where Don Julian got all these dolls and what kind of love was given to them by their living hosts? For all we know, it could be a network of spirits there who seek love from a human. Maybe the spirits possess the dolls in order to find a kid who gives her love to a doll and in turn gives her love to a spirit. So many possibilities...

For that episode, I brought along Harold the Haunted Doll to see if it could open up a connection with the spirits on the island. I totally regret it. This doll has been connected to death on several occasions and has bounced from family to family over the years because no one wants to keep it. I'll never forget picking up that doll in Mexico and then feeling my arm start to itch like it was on fire. Not long after, I developed three bruises the size of fingerprints on my left arm (the one that picked it up).

The psychic medium had told us not to touch the doll or we could lose our own limbs, just like the doll was losing its left arm. We did anyway (go figure). When we took Harold out of his case, cats went crazy, and other dolls suddenly started laughing. With

Harold the Haunted Doll.

no electrical source at all, they laughed! On a thermal camera, we documented unexplainable heat coming off of Harold when we put him in a shed on the island. It was absolutely nuts. If anything from my travels gives me bad dreams, it's the Island of the Dolls and Harold the Haunted Doll.

Just thinking about this makes me feel uneasy, and talking about Harold and the island creeps me out like nothing else. That investigation is the most difficult one of my career to speak about. It's 40 degrees in Vegas as I'm writing this chapter, and I'm sweating. If you ever see me in public, don't pick a fight with me, because you'll get one. But come up to me with a bunch of dolls taped to your body and I'll run like a girl.

I'M DONE.

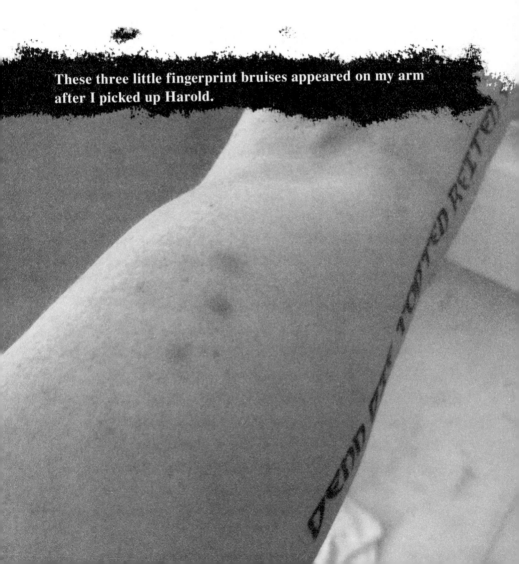

These three little fingerprint bruises appeared on my arm after I picked up Harold.

16

WEATHER

It's a bigger part of the paranormal than you think.

I believe that when a person dies and his or her soul remains on Earth for whatever reason, the soul becomes intertwined with the electromagnetic and geomagnetic forces of the planet. Under the right conditions, these forces, along with certain weather events, can enable spirits to manifest and be seen by the living. Even with all the tools and data we have at our disposal, the weather can be unpredictable and trick us, just as the manifestation of spirits seems random and unpredictable. But it doesn't have to be. I believe that the two are interconnected, and that just as we can predict the weather with a lot of accuracy, someday we will be able to predict apparitions and sightings. We just have to understand all the variables and be in the right place at the right time when all the factors line up.

I hate to make this analogy, but if you remember the movie *Ghostbusters,* then you remember the green slime left behind by the movie ghosts. Like those Hollywood ghosts, I think people leave behind a residual energy after an extremely emotional event, but it's more like a burn mark on a wood wall after a fire. This residue contains the emotions of the event, and certain meteorological conditions can reignite it. It's like a combination lock that's opened when certain conditions are met. What is the combination of climatic conditions that opens this lock? That's the million-dollar question!

When we investigated the Old Charleston Jail in Charleston, South Carolina, we captured the wails and cries of inmates who were tortured there. I believe this is the residue of their emotional lives and/or deaths being unlocked under certain conditions. Think about the Stone Tape Theory that I described in chapter 14, "Carrying Spirits," which says that certain materials (such as sandstone or silica) can store life events and replay them the same way a cassette tape records and plays back music. The circumstances of release are usually consistent, meaning that the stone lets go of the event at certain times of day and maybe even under certain weather conditions.

This theory has some validity when you consider that iron oxide is the main component of audiotape. Iron oxide is everywhere, and the Earth's core is made mostly of iron and nickel. It also has been proven that certain crystals, like quartz and silicon, can retain information and are found almost everywhere, even within some rocks. Computer chips used to store data are made from silicon, which is the second most abundant element on the planet next to oxygen and is found in almost every form of rock. So it's not a stretch to imagine that certain natural materials can store traumatic and emotional events and release them when the conditions are right.

Maybe it's the weather that unlocks these events that are stored in natural materials. When the barometric pressure, humidity level, temperature, moon phase, and even running water (which increases electromagnetic activity) connect in the right way, I believe that the residue of someone's life can be released in the form of audio and visual presentations. Voices and apparitions could be triggered by environmental elements when they synchronize, possibly when they match up with the weather conditions that were present at the time of the emotional event (like the death of a loved one).

Of course, this would indicate that the residue is not an intelligent spirit; it's only a moment of a life recorded by natural materials and released under certain conditions. It's a moment in time captured and played back like a cassette tape or computer chip. It's just stored energy unlocked by the weather.

So how does the weather react with intelligent spirits? First, think about spirits and why they are here. I believe spirits that don't move on to the next life either didn't pass God's judgment or have unresolved issues that keep them earthbound. That means they're

There's a connection between the paranormal and the weather that we need to decipher.

angry or confused and therefore want to be heard. They gather their energy to move objects and communicate, which sometimes means that they attack humans to get the attention they crave. When they can't gather energy through electronic means (like stealing energy from computers, light fixtures, camera equipment, or whatever), they turn to weather phenomena to get the boost they need. I've seen this happen during investigations.

Remember the attacks at the Exorcist House that I described in chapter 11, "Heart Attacks"? Nick and I had a spirit box session during which a voice presented itself as "Diablo" twice and gave us some other information in a short span of time. Shortly afterward, Aaron went back into the room where we captured the voice and got very dizzy and felt intense heat. At the same time, Bill Chappell (who's an amazing engineer) monitored a sensor that measured weather data in the house, and he said that there was a sudden increase in humidity when this happened to Aaron. It was around dusk, a time of day when there should be a decrease in humidity, not an increase. We were baffled because a strange weather phenomenon was happening at the exact same time as paranormal activity, but we couldn't find the connection between the two.

During other investigations, passing storms affected the level of paranormal activity we captured. I'll never forget when we were investigating the Hales-Bar Dam in Tennessee and a massive storm raged through, bringing a tornado that tossed an entire dock full of boats onto the shore (and us along with them!). That evening we caught an amazing image of an apparition manifesting on a thermal imaging camera—a rare event. We capture voices, EVPs, orbs, and other paranormal activity all the time, but an apparition is unusual, and this one appeared within a few hours of a massive lightning storm. I believe that it's possible for the discharge of electricity into the atmosphere (in the form of lightning) to give spirits the extra energy they need to feed off of and manifest.

I like to use movie analogies when I talk about the paranormal because it makes things easier for people to relate to. (I'm a cinephile. What can I say?) There's a scene in *Total Recall* where the humans on Mars are dependent on giant fans to keep them going. When the fans slow down, the humans get sluggish and weak, and when the fans speed up, so does life. I believe that spirits are the same way. When the weather is calm, they don't have anything to energize them, but when there's electricity in the air, they have an energy source to draw from and can manifest. I'm sure there's more to it than that, but we don't have the raw data to prove it...yet.

In some places the weather is unreliable, and spirits have to find other forms of energy. Hydroelectric plants and flowing water are proven conductors of electromagnetic energy, so sites like that usually see a higher than average level of paranormal activity. The Rolling Hills Asylum in New York, which is just across the street from an electric power plant that puts out kajillions of volts of power, is one of the most active places I've ever been. We captured every form of paranormal evidence there, all in the same night. I think this plant powered more than just the local houses. Everything that contains life contains energy, and ghosts are attracted to that energy. I think they're even more dependent on energy than we are.

Think about this: We are surrounded by cosmic waves. They bombard the Earth every day, but we can't see or hear them. Every scientist in the world will agree that the waves are there, but they're invisible. Except for one area: the high latitudes where they collide with the magnetosphere. We call the light they create the aurora borealis, and no one can deny that it exists because it's visible to the naked eye when the conditions are right.

So why can't ghosts be the same way? If they're made up of electromagnetic energy, then what weather conditions cause that electromagnetic energy to strengthen? Dusk? Moving water? High temperature? Low humidity? Solar radiation? I'm sure there's a connection, but the only way to prove it is to study the meteorological conditions that were present when every major piece of paranormal evidence was collected. Going back to do so for past events is impossible, but that could (and should) be a study of its own for future paranormal researchers.

I would like to see every paranormal team out there start recording more weather data when they collect evidence. Maybe if we did that, we could spot trends and do real research. Maybe if we knew that 90 percent of the time when a ghost manifests, the humidity is below 75 percent, the temperature is above 60 degrees, and the time of day is between 7 and 11 pm, then we could start doing real predictive analysis. Maybe if we knew that there was a strong coronal eruption or sunspot 90 percent of the time when EVPs are captured, then we could connect the two and even theorize that solar eruptions (which flood the Earth with energy) give spirits the strength they need to communicate. We can't just keep walking through the darkness in isolated teams trying to bump into things. We need to make the spirits come to us, or at least use our data to predict when and where they'll be. Then people will look at paranormal investigators just like they do weather forecasters.

MAYBE I'LL EVEN GET MY OWN TV SHOW...

17

A Savage Attack in a Peaceful Place

The California coast has some dark secrets.

Living in Las Vegas can drain a man's soul. The transient party people, the massive temperature swings, the oppressive energy, the repeated attacks on friends in my home by dark spirits…it wears me down sometimes. Two years ago, I realized that nothing was going well here. I felt that my environment was having an effect on me, and I knew I needed to get away. I sought a change somewhere, anywhere—a refuge from the neon lights and the "what happens in Vegas stays in Vegas" attitude.

But I was also committed to filming *Ghost Adventures,* and I knew I couldn't get away to some remote mountaintop cut off from the civilized world. It had to be near reliable transportation hubs and Internet connections so I could collaborate with my producers and crew on filming and editing the episodes. I didn't want to get away from my life as much as I wanted to escape my town.

One day my mother mentioned Monterey, California. I had never been there, but I'd heard of Carmel and knew it was pretty close by, so I looked it up. I discovered that Monterey, Carmel, and Pacific Grove all lie on a tiny, unique peninsula. The whole area looked like a different world, and I was immediately captivated. Because of the way the valley is formed and the prevailing winds blow, the temperature stays in the 60s in the summer. It looked foggy, damp, and beautiful and reminded me of Scotland's medieval craggy cliffs, but it was right here in the U.S. I was sold. I'm not a spontaneous person, but something about it called me there. I booked a ticket and flew out the next day. I knew that I wasn't going to see Vegas for a while, and it felt good.

I landed, booked a room in a small resort near the water, and was lost for words. This was exactly what I needed. It was quiet. It was relaxing. It was therapeutic. I could feel the knots in my soul untying themselves. But it wasn't cheap, and I racked up the hotel time. I make a good living, but I'm not what you call an impulsive spender or splurger. If I was going to stay a while, I needed to rent a house that was more economical, but like the spirits I encounter, the sticker shock of the California coast followed me. The only reasonable place I could find was a Grandma cottage that had honey pots painted with bees in tutus displayed on worn-out shelves. It was rustic and old, and though it wasn't really me, it was a hundred yards from the beach, and the misty, mossy, dramatic coastline was the perfect place for a man who wants to lead the life of Dracula.

The Monterey Peninsula had its hooks in me, and I was enjoying it too much to leave, so I rented the cottage for a month, moved my stuff in, and tried to figure out why this place had called me there. Because it did. I rarely (if ever) just pack up and leave. I plan my trips, especially when I'm going to be gone for a long time, but I also firmly believe that things happen for a reason. Forces beyond flesh and blood guide me to certain places, and something brought me here without a second thought. Something more than just my mother's suggestion.

I couldn't sit around and do nothing all day, so I did some research on the area and learned about its history. I took a drive to Pacific Grove, whose Victorian homes with plaques stating the names of the families that built them in the 1800s made it seem more like Europe than America to me. It had a sense of history, of a bygone era, that I haven't seen much on the West Coast.

Next I visited the Carmel Mission and met a priest named Juniper Serra who was an expert on the area. The Carmel Mission was so similar to the La Purisma Mission that we investigated in 2009 that I felt an immediate connection to it. La Purisma was such a powerful place that it became a part of me, and the Carmel Mission was damn near its twin, so I went there often to unwind and heal from all the negative energy I'd accumulated. My soul felt like a wet mop full of dirty water that needed to be wrung out.

It didn't take long to hear the stories of the hauntings there. Like La Purisma, the graveyard at the Carmel Mission was equal parts Native American graves and graves of the men who had journeyed there as Catholic missionaries. The ground was saturated with the histories and energies of the multitudes who had come before us, but it wasn't negative. In fact, it was the polar opposite of the gates of hell; it was more like the stairway to heaven. It was refreshing, so I went there every day until something else demanded my attention.

I developed a routine in Carmel: I would wake up, get my hot tea, put my dog Gracie on her leash, walk toward the ocean, let my

FUN FACT:

AFTER I LEFT CARMEL, FATHER SERRA SENT ME AN INCREDIBLE VIDEO THAT CAPTURED AN APPARITION ON FILM INSIDE THE MISSION.

mind go blank, and then turn toward town. There are no addresses on the houses, so it's easy to get lost. One otherwise normal day, I took a new turn for no real reason, and then another and another. I wasn't worried about being lost; in fact, I remember thinking, "Wherever we end up is where we end up." Suddenly I looked up and saw an old medieval-looking castle staring back at me. The fog hovered over its tall tower, but instead of being frightened, I felt like it was inviting me in to learn more. I didn't fight it.

I walked toward the tower with no care whatsoever about whether it was private property, and Gracie and I stood at the front gate and stared. I felt like something was looking back at me. A sign said "Tor House," so I made a note of it and decided to come back later to explore it.

I learned that the poet Robinson Jeffers built the Tor House by hand in 1919 and then built the adjoining Hawk Tower between 1920 and 1924. It's an impressive structure, even more impressive when you consider that he built it by himself with only some aid from a local stonemason. Jeffers wasn't trained in construction, but he managed to build the place by himself while he was one of the leading poets of his time. That's talent.

I was never one for poetry or literature or even reading books until I met Vince Huth, a stately gentleman who serves as president of the Tor House Foundation. I set up a tour (of the Tor House—pun intended), and when Huth met me at the front door, he immediately started reading a poem by Jeffers called…wait for it…*Ghost*.

As he read it, I felt an incredible sense of destiny, because in the poem a man walking his dog outside the house encounters the spirit of Robinson Jeffers examining the mortar-joints. That was me, Jeffers was there, and I was chilled to the bone. Even more shocking was how the poem states that fifty years would pass before this happened, and I was there on the fiftieth anniversary of Jeffers' death.

This was no coincidence; it was meant to be.

These are the types of experiences that define my life—how ghosts, spirits, demons, and supernatural powers guide me on this journey. This is why *Ghost Adventures* is more than just a TV show.

Gracie and I at the Tor House.

Ghost Adventures is the journey of my life as I interact with things most people cannot see, feel, or understand. The ghosts choose the locations for us, not the other way around. I believe Robinson Jeffers was in touch with the spiritual plane while he was alive and spirits guided him to build the Tor House. He was one with the stones and knew that he and his wife would remain there after their deaths. And he knew that one day he would bring me to it.

We ended up filming an episode at the Tor House, which was the third location in the area that I became interested in during my several-month stay. (The others were the Brookdale Lodge in Santa Cruz and the Point Sur Lighthouse in Big Sur.) As you can imagine, the investigation was a powerful one for me. Robinson Jeffers' poetry integrated itself into our work and helped define us as we helped define Jeffers. It was as if he had predicted our visit, and it ended up being one of the most personal investigations ever for me.

While I was using the SB7 spirit box on the very bed where Jeffers died, a voice came through and said "ghost"—the name of the poem that had brought me there and predicted this moment. I believe that this voice belonged to Jeffers himself, and I communicated him and his wife, Una. She conducted séances in the house and tower, which was the first thing I saw through the fog that day Gracie and I stumbled upon them. She spoke to us through the spirit box and said, "Welcome to my..." I never could make out the last word, but the other three were clear. I believe that Robinson Jeffers built this place out of rock in order to house his and his wife's spirits after death, as he wrote about in his poems.

People watch *Ghost Adventures* because they want to be scared or entertained, but it has a deeper meaning, as the episode about the Tor House illustrates. When you watch it, watch deeper. You'll see the passion that brought us there, and you'll understand why the ghosts guided us to them. It's not some random place we wanted to film at for three days before moving on to the next one.

Even the most wonderful locations can turn terrifying, though. It happened to me during the Monterey investigations, and I was totally unprepared for it.

After we finished filming at the Tor House, we went straight to the Point Sur Lighthouse just down the coast. After the first day of filming there, we realized that the level of paranormal activity was intense—more intense than we thought it would be, to be honest. Over time, the lighthouse has witnessed countless shipwrecks within just a few hundred yards, and multiple investigators have captured disembodied voices and EVPs there. It's as if the lighthouse signals spirits the same way it signaled ships on the ocean, and they flock to it.

I had just come off of a positive spiritual investigation at the Tor House. I'd done a full day of interviews at the lighthouse, and I was really tired. I went back to "Grandma's cottage" and got ready for bed. I was downstairs getting something to eat, alone except for Gracie and the bee jars, when I heard a boom upstairs in my bedroom, followed by loud scratching noises on the floor. I ran up there and found my clothes scattered all over the place, like something you would see in a cop drama when gangsters ransack a room looking for a safe. Something was up. Something bad. I could feel it. Looking back on it, I should have left the house right then, but of course I didn't.

The clothes couldn't have made the boom noise, and there were no giant raccoons in the room to make the scratching sounds; there was no way for a critter to get in or out. I was disturbed and uncomfortable, but too tired to worry about it. I've faced some pretty evil stuff, so I dismissed it, cleaned up, and lay down to sleep...but never got the chance.

Lying in bed, I was startled by banging noises followed by the feeling of hands on my shoulders. Something grabbed me and pinned me down against the headboard. It didn't move me, but held me still with enough force that I knew I wasn't going to be able to move until it wanted me to. I struggled, but it was too strong.

This was no sleep paralysis. I was on my back, my eyes were open, and I was yelling. Something physically held me down for about twenty seconds, and while it did, I heard more banging noises in the room. It was one of the most disturbing feelings I've ever felt. A burst of negative energy attacked me not with bumps or scratches, but with a transfusion of horrific violent energy. It was powerful, and to be honest, I was scared.

Finally it released me, but I was shaking so badly that I couldn't move. The room was forty degrees colder—no exaggeration. The attack was so sudden and severe that I called Billy and Aaron and screamed at them to come over, my voice and hands shaking. I should have run, but I couldn't leave the room. The spirit was still there, and it wouldn't let me go. I was a hostage in that cottage.

Billy and Aaron raced over, ran upstairs, and felt it immediately. They knew that something was in the room, and it gave me a strange comfort to know that I wasn't the only one who could sense it. They grabbed me and took me downstairs, and the three of us (and Gracie) peeled rubber, leaving all the lights on behind us. I booked a room in their hotel and stayed there, refusing to spend another minute in that cottage.

I knew the force that had held me down was the same dark energy that had made the loud noise and thrown my clothes everywhere, but I didn't feel like it was attached to the house. I'd been staying in this cottage for weeks and nothing had happened. So where did it come from? Did it follow me from Point Sur or the Tor House? If it did, why? And what was it trying to tell me—to get out of town or to stop my investigations there? It was the strangest transfusion of pure hell that I've ever known, which is weird because none of those locations are known to contain dark or demonic entities. It didn't make sense then and doesn't make sense now.

Despite this attack, I treasure the time I spent in California. Robinson Jeffers' spirit called me there, and I'm glad I listened, because I got the chance to tell his story and have an encounter like no other. I finally went home to Vegas and moved back into my house, my spirit refreshed and my life in a little more order than it had been. When I think about how everyone says, "What happens in Vegas stays in Vegas," I find it ironic. For me, what happened in California stayed in California.

UNTIL NOW.

18

ST. JAMES HOTEL

The show must go on.

There are days when you say, "I'm dying," in a joking way, and then there are days when you actually believe that you may be on your last legs. When we traveled to Cimarron, New Mexico, to investigate the St. James Hotel, I was so sick that I honestly felt like I was dying—like one of those cases of pneumonia you hear about that eventually takes someone's life. I could barely remember my name, let alone focus on an interview. When I eventually did do the interview, I swayed like a drunkard. I didn't know what I had, but it was hell.

When we travel to film in some of these haunted locations, there's nothing else around. It's scary sometimes when one of us gets sick or ill, because there's no urgent care in these remote areas. I've done investigations in faraway places that were hours from any kind of healthcare. If you slipped while rappelling down an old mineshaft, you'd be screwed. I learned long ago not to take unnecessary risks like that or to put myself in a position that could cause permanent injury so far from civilization.

In the middle of New Mexico, Cimarron is three hours from the nearest major city (Denver to the north and Albuquerque to the south). It has a population of around 900 people, so there's no real hospital to speak of. I was sick and needed medicine, and the future of the episode was in jeopardy, so we drove north to Trinidad, Colorado, which we later learned is the sex change capital of the world.

FUN FACT:

DR. STANLEY BIBER STARTED CONDUCTING SEX REASSIGNMENT SURGERY IN THE 1960S IN TRINIDAD AND GAINED A REPUTATION FOR BEING VERY GOOD AT IT. AT HIS PEAK, HE PERFORMED UP TO FOUR OPERATIONS PER DAY. HIS PRACTICE WAS SO WELL KNOWN THAT BIBER WAS FEATURED IN AN EPISODE OF *SOUTH PARK*.

We found this little health food store that was selling herbal oil remedies passed down through generations of Native Americans. When we went in, we were like three city slickers walking into the High Noon Saloon in Dodge City in 1888. The music stopped. Heads turned. I felt uneasy, even through all the pounding in my head and the hummingbirds in my stomach that wouldn't stop fluttering. A bad situation quickly got worse, but it wasn't me everyone was wary of.

Aaron, with his bald head, goatee, and hoodie, was singled out as the criminal of the group, and the locals watched him like a hawk. We browsed the store, and while I was looking for anything that would make the golems in my gut go away, everyone watched Aaron. I hated that, but I bought a bunch of tinctures in glass bottles because at that point I would have tried anything to get better. We got back in the car, and I threw back shots of these oils, the smell of which made all of us sick. Every time my body would try to heave up the oils, I would force them back down, because in the back of my mind I thought, *This is the only option I have. There's nowhere else to go for healthcare around here.* I felt like I was back in medieval times subject to ancient natural cures, and none of them worked. It was awful.

The thing about being a TV show host is that the show must go on. If I'm down, then it's a domino effect; it costs more money, more problems, and more headaches for everyone if I can't do my job. The network has deadlines and a lot of people were counting on me, so I had to push through it. In television, no one cares how sick or distracted or dead to the world you are; you have to find the strength to pull yourself up by the bootstraps and accomplish your mission. In the military they call this FIDO: Fuck It, Drive On.

As I've said, my buddies and production crew are my family, especially when I'm at my worst. My production manager kept bringing me water, and the guys kept asking if there was anything they could do. We've built camaraderie like I imagine a platoon of soldiers would in combat. These are your brothers, and they're all you have out there in the middle of nowhere.

The worst part for me is that I'm a perfectionist. I want to deliver the best show, the best interviews, the best investigation. I won't settle for anything less. That's why I'm the leader of *Ghost Adventures*. I constantly push Nick, Aaron, and everyone on our production crew to do better and make each show better than the last.

So when I'm down, I don't like it. It makes me feel insecure about my performance as a host and as a paranormal investigator, because I know that the product everyone will see, which represents me, my crew, and the Travel Channel, is not going to be as good as it could be. Is that micromanaging? Maybe, but *Ghost Adventures* is my life, and the show's reputation is a direct reflection on me and all the people who believe in me, so it's my responsibility to get it right. I had to fight through the pain to deliver a great investigation.

It ended up being a great episode, but that wasn't the last of it. After the investigation was over, we piled into an RV that we had rented because the site was so far from civilization and headed back to the town we were staying in, which was about forty minutes away. We were exhausted. I was physically sick, mentally drained from coming in contact with several spirits that night, and ready to collapse. Aaron was sleeping in the cabin above the driver, and I was propped up like a scarecrow in between and just behind the driver and passenger. I should have gone to sleep on one of the benches, but for some reason I couldn't. I think the events of the investigation were still running through my head, or maybe the most recent episode of *Game of Thrones* was on my mind. Either way, my head was still in the game, but only in short bursts. I droned in and out of consciousness as we drove until...

"Oh my God!" the driver yelled, snapping me awake and scaring the crap out of me. I've faced some dangerous beastly spirits in my life, but this startled me pretty badly. What the hell was going on?

An elk. Or a moose. I really don't know which it was, but I'm guessing it was an elk since moose rarely wander that far south. Either way, it was huge. And not just one, but two. And then...a lot more. A herd. A herd of giant animals was standing in the middle of the road in the earliest hours of the morning, staring at us. The message in their eyes was clear: "No, *you* move."

It was what I imagine an acid trip must be like. Giant elk—or moose or reindeer or Sasquatches for all I knew, I was so sick and tired—were standing on a road in a remote part of northern New Mexico, blocking our path. It was blacker than black. No moon. Our headlights reflected off of them, and we finally inched our way around the herd and got moving again.

The danger seemingly behind us, I started to doze off again, but what do you think happened minutes later? "Oh my God!" our driver screamed again. I looked up and saw another huge beast trying to cross the road in front of us. We were going too fast to stop in the road like we had for the herd, so the driver swerved left to avoid this 1,000-pound animal, but couldn't. The elk hit the passenger side of the RV, and I'll never forget the sound it made. Please keep in mind that I'm an advocate for animal rights; I've adopted pets and donated tens of thousands of dollars to animal shelters over the course of my life. So hearing the dull thud of a majestic beast hitting the side of our RV at 60 miles per hour and knowing that the blow was probably fatal sickens me to this day.

The right side of the RV that juts out just behind the passenger seat had caught the elk's head. Had the animal been a few feet farther into the road, it might have come through the windshield and injured Nick. We immediately slowed down and stopped about 100 feet from the impact site, all of us dumbfounded about what had just happened.

As we turned around to go back, we saw chunks of flesh in the road, and I knew what the fate of this elk must be. There was no way it could have survived. But as we got closer to the impact point, we saw it on the side of the road. I'll be honest, I was a little afraid to get out, because elk and moose are known to bum-rush people and stampede them, and we had just seen a herd not ten minutes before. How many more of them were out there in the darkness just off the road?

We all mustered up the courage to get out and check on the animal only to find our worst fears confirmed. It was still alive, but with half of its head missing. Chunks of its back were also torn away, and it was trying to get up but couldn't. We all felt like shit; I was not only sick to my stomach, but also dejected. We knew we had to either save it or put it out of its misery, but we didn't have cell phone reception or a gun. Hunters do their best to get a clean kill so the animal doesn't suffer, and I wanted to show this beast the same respect, but we couldn't find any sort of rock or tool to do the job. We sat there for twenty minutes, a group of adults with the mental capacity of kids watching *Old Yeller*. We had no choice but to leave. People may think that's cruel, but how many motorists actually stop and go back to check on the animal they hit? At least we did that, even if we couldn't help it.

I had gone to Cimarron feeling like I was going to die, but determined to push through it no matter what the cost. I never imagined that the cost would be the life of an incredible and innocent animal.

SHOW BUSINESS.

19

OVERLAND HOTEL

The most painful investigation ever.

We're all born with features we don't like: toes that curl under, droopy jowls, unibrows, whatever. Nobody's perfect, unless you're Paris Hilton. Wait—she has gigantic clown feet. (I don't hate her, but she treated a friend of mine like shit when he tried to help her, so…I'll leave it there.)

I've had the hardest time breathing since I can remember. My septum is deviated, which Wikipedia says is "an abnormal condition in which the top of the cartilaginous ridge leans to the left or the right, causing obstruction of the affected nasal passage. The condition can result in poor drainage of the sinuses. Patients can also complain of difficulty breathing, headaches, bloody noses, or sleeping disorders such as snoring or sleep apnea."

Yep, that's me. The condition has made many facets of life difficult, so I've always wanted to correct it. I don't get into the "changing yourself through surgery is wrong" argument that some people like to throw around. It's your body. If you're unhappy with it and you can afford to change it, then it's up to you, not the people who disapprove for their own moral reasons. Of course I also believe that we have to live with the consequences of our actions, so if you pay some cheap, uncertified doctor to give you a boob job and end up with tennis balls under your armpits, then you can't complain when someone stares at you in a bikini with curiosity rather than admiration.

I wanted to get my nose worked on for a long time, but always out of necessity. I don't think it ever looked bad, but it wasn't efficient. I never breathed well and always wanted to. So I bit the bullet. Now that it's done, I'm much more comfortable, but the pain of surgery was way more than I expected. If you're a hater and want to hear a story of me in severe pain, then this chapter is for you.

There were plenty of things about the surgery that scared me. First, I have a fear of anesthesia. I'm kind of a control freak, and being put under is a total relinquishing of control that makes me nervous. Putting your life in the hands of others isn't easy. Does that mean I have trust issues? Probably.

Second, the pain. Let's not beat around the bush here. Even the toughest man in the world feels the searing agony of being sliced and diced, and having your nose cut open and rearranged doesn't exactly tickle. I was assured that there would be severe discomfort for several weeks afterward, but from everything I'd read, it was worth it. Breathing is rather crucial to life, after all, so I weighed the risks and decided to go for it. I knew it would test me, and I was confident that I would pass.

I called a local plastic surgeon named Lane Smith. I didn't think I'd be able to find one in Vegas, but he looked professional and... dare I say it...trustworthy? When I went in for a consultation, the office was full of *Ghost Adventures* fans. That was cool, but I digress. I'm usually a proactive person, but some things you just go for and don't think about. When I see something and am sure it's what I want or need, I get it. I don't wait. After meeting with Dr.

Smith for an hour, I felt good enough about the procedure that I plodded forward and went all in.

We set a date for two weeks later, and the doctor prescribed some medications for me to take before I came in. That's when shit got serious. If I ever had a chance to chicken out, that was it, so I had him charge me for the surgery beforehand. I figured that if I paid for it then and there, my cold feet would be kept warm.

The night before the surgery, I couldn't sleep. I took a Valium and lay in bed staring at the ceiling, thinking through all the things that could go wrong. Like flying, I could envision all the disasters but none of the safe landings. The next morning, as my mother drove me to the clinic, I freaked out and texted Billy and Aaron a thousand jokes to make myself feel better. I was scared, I admit it. The drive to the clinic was worse than the drive to a lockdown.

I had to put on that stupid hospital gown and sit in a room by myself, alone with my thoughts. So many times in my life, spirits have come to me when I didn't want them to, but in my hour of extreme loneliness, they were nowhere to be found. Ironic.

Finally it was time. I walked down the hall dragging an IV bag on wheels, my gown flapping open in the back. Anyone who's ever wanted to see my bare ass missed their opportunity that day. The anesthesiologist told me to lie down and put on some music. It was good, and I was calm. I remember I was...

Boom! I woke up. Had I fallen asleep for a second? I wasn't sure. "Where am I? When are we doing the surgery?" I asked.

"We already did it," the nurse responded.

I think I asked her the same question three times, but she kept saying, "You were under for three hours. It's over." I literally lost my mind. I couldn't get a grip on anything, and for a guy who holds on so tightly to life, this was maddening. Panic ensued. My blood pressure skyrocketed. Then I heard my mom's voice and began to realize that I had to calm down.

I vaguely remembered the doctor telling me about this possibility in our pre-operation meeting. He warned me about those rare patients who come out of anesthesia and go apeshit trying to get control of themselves. I guess that rare guy is me, and fortunately they don't take it personally, because I said things I don't want to repeat. I'll be sending those nurses flowers forever as an apology.

I got into the car with my mother and we left to go home, but we had to make a few stops on the way. Disgusting stuff was oozing from my nose. If you saw any of it on the side of the road, you'd swear that a zombie had been killed, skinned, and gutted there.

For the next three days I did absolutely nothing. For the first time in years, I had no work, no stress, no nothing. Looking back, I'm glad for it, but it was also more boring than watching C-SPAN. Facial surgery isn't like surgery on another part of the body. Because it's on your face, it's impossible to put out of your mind. All you can do is be in pain and think about the pain and try to breathe through the pain and wish there wasn't any more pain and hope the pain will be worth it someday. I had no one to blame but myself, though: I had pain medications but didn't take them. Like I said before, I hate feeling out of control, and painkillers and psychotropic drugs are designed to do just that: take the control away from you. No thanks. All I had were some antibiotics and my own thoughts.

On the fourth day, the spirits finally visited. I could feel them in the room with me, and all I could think was, *Where have you been?* I wasn't really in the mood to be around them, so I shut them out. Nothing personal, but I think there comes a point in everyone's life when social interaction is a nuisance. Even ethereal beings can be intruders sometimes.

Just after surgery.

The worst pain was getting the stitches removed. The nurses used pliers to pluck these fishing lines from my nose, and for fuck's sake it hurt. I actually screamed, and I contemplated taking pain drugs for the first time. This was no small surgery. I have a big schnoz. It was like chopping down a redwood tree and piecing it back together with pliers.

The day after the bandages were removed, I did exactly what the doctor told me not to do: I went back to work. I've always done things my way, and on this one I decided that taking a risk was worthwhile. After all, a lot of people depend on me to tough out the hard times and get the job done. I did listen to the doctor a little bit, though. He told me not to fly for several weeks after the surgery, so we picked a location within driving distance of Vegas and headed to Pioche, Nevada, to investigate the Overland Hotel. But right away things went wrong.

I was still in pain. Lots of it. And my desire not to take strong pain meds wasn't helping. The last thing I want to do is look drunk on film, so all I took was Tylenol. The simple act of walking and feeling the cold air hitting my nose hurt—that's how sensitive it was. I'm a tough guy, but filming this episode was going to be a challenge with a swollen face and a nose that would bleed without warning. I feared it would start dripping just as we caught a piece of evidence, and people would try to link an EVP or apparition to my bleeding nose and freak out. I didn't want my nose to get any attention and was trying hard to conceal what I was going through, but if it suddenly started to bleed while we were on camera capturing paranormal evidence, then I would have to address it. My solution was to buy a cowboy hat and wear it really low, but I couldn't hide my voice. I sounded like Lurch from *The Addams Family*.

The first day in Pioche it was hard to concentrate. My nose felt worse than it should have, and I started to wonder if I should go back to Vegas and see the doctor. I had never had major surgery before and had never gone under anesthesia, so I think my entire body was trying to recover, not just my nose. The doctor's order to stay home and take it easy echoed in my head, and a few of the events that followed made me wonder why I hadn't heeded his warning.

We were filming an interview in a cemetery with a man named Jim Kelley who was an expert on the history of the area. Before the interview I noticed that he had a gun in his holster, so I got the idea that he should shoot me in the back as I walked away. The gun was full of blanks, so I thought it would be good for dramatic effect, but as we were doing the interview I was hurting. Every time my foot hit the ground, it would vibrate up through my body and shoot pain into my nose. I wished that someone had invented pillow shoes for this very situation. I had second thoughts about Jim shooting me, but finally decided "the hell with it." The show must go on, right?

As I turned to leave, Jim did as promised and popped off a couple of blanks into my back. It was loud—way louder than I expected. And I felt the sparks from the gun hit my back. I stumbled forward and found myself in total agony. Just taking a few unexpected steps caused me immense pain, and my nose instantly started bleeding. Every second felt like a year until I was finally stable and standing still again, but then I got a little worried. Did the sudden jerking motion jack up the surgery, and would I have to return to Vegas to see the doctor immediately? It felt like it. We ended up using this shot in a brief reenactment that you see for only a second, because it just didn't go off very well.

I toughed it out, but the rest of the shoot was hell. That moment caused a ripple effect over the next few days. I spent a lot of that shoot in my hotel room. I had strep throat when we filmed at the Riddle House, and my throat looked like it had a golf ball in it, but this pain was far worse. When you have pain in the center of your face that shoots down your nerves, it will drive you crazy, and several times I had to force myself to keep working.

When we arrived for the lockdown, I was trying to move very softly. Again, pillow shoes. Wish I had some. The funny thing was, I thought it was going to be a calm shoot, but it ended up being one of the most insanely active lockdowns ever—maybe even in the top three in the history of *Ghost Adventures*. Upstairs the spirits were extremely active, and we were all on edge, but it was an ordinary phenomenon that would have the biggest impact on me.

Have you ever seen those plug-in air fresheners that spray out a mist every seven minutes and make a loud hissing noise? Well, in the middle of the night during an active paranormal investigation, they're very unwelcome. I was walking down the hall when one suddenly hissed and I felt the spray hit my face. I yelled and jumped, and again that motion killed my nose. The surgeon's words echoed in my head: "Don't make any sudden movements for two weeks after the cast is off, or you will jeopardize everything. You may even cause a blood clot." The air freshener caused the second big jolt I'd had in Pioche, and it hurt so badly that we had to take a break from filming so I could sit down to let the pain subside.

Later that night, we were getting great evidence from the spirit box when I felt something shoot through me. It was an amazing force, and I fell backward and hit the ground. You know what happened next: pain. Intense, shooting pain, like I'd been shot in the face with a flamethrower. This didn't last for three minutes; it lasted for three days. As soon as I got back to Vegas, I went to the doctor to get checked out. Thankfully, everything was fine, and a few weeks later I was back to feeling like myself.

I was unprepared for that powerful moment, and I wasn't able to really dive into it to figure out what it was. Normally I would have tried to get more interaction with the spirit, but I was down for the count. I shouldn't have put myself and everyone counting on me in that position, but I did. It was an amazing paranormal moment, but if I had been 100 percent, I wonder what else we could have learned from that encounter. I'm definitely not done with that place; I intend to go back.

In the end, having the surgery was definitely the right decision, and my message to anyone considering plastic surgery is to weigh the risks and rewards carefully. I didn't have surgery to make myself look better, but to help me breathe better, and it has. I'm much happier and healthier now that I get more oxygen into my system. My voice is different now, and recording voice-overs has been a hell of a challenge (we usually record them after shooting an episode), but when it's all said and done, the pain was worth it.

Ironically, we caught a voice on the spirit box at the Overland Hotel that said, "I need my medicine."

I FEEL YA, BROTHER. I FEEL YA.

20

DREAMS

Why I have a true fear of clowns.

Do you remember any of the nightmares you had as a preschooler? I do. Between the ages of three and five, I had too many nightmares to recall. And not just your run-of-the-mill kid nightmares, either—these were scary, visceral visions that still haunt me to this day. They were so vivid and detailed that I would wake up and not know whether I was still in the dream.

I don't know how someone that young could have such violent, terror-inducing nightmares that were so memorable, but it happened to me. I'd never seen violent TV, been exposed to violent video games, or watched the news to see the myriad ways people hurt each other—so how could I have known such fear? To be afraid of something, you have to be aware of the possible consequences. To be afraid of flying, for example, you have to know that a crash can result in gruesome death. At five years old, what did I know about the world that could have caused me true fear? Nothing. And yet many nights I was terrified to go to sleep.

They say that nightmares are often based on something you see or hear just before going to sleep, like a terrible news story or a horror movie. Traumatic life events can cause nightmares for years, and some people never get over them. I didn't experience any trauma growing up, so I don't know what could have triggered these awful nights. I was less than five years old but was dreaming about things that would make a middle-aged man cower in fear.

One of my most persistent dreams involved clowns, but let's put that one on hold for a moment. There was another dream that's just as significant. It involved a man breaking into our house, and I'll never forget it. This evil guy would hold my hands so I couldn't move them and then stick sewing needles into my hands as far as they could go, one after the other. I would scream and cry and feel that pain. My mom and sister couldn't find me—like we lived in a maze like the Winchester Mystery House, but it was still our house—yet I could hear them screaming for me as I screamed for them. I still think about that dream and try to decipher it. When I left Florida and moved to Chicago and then Detroit, I left my mom and sister behind and entered into the darkest period of my life. I felt a lot of pain, and things went very badly. Now that we all live in Las Vegas, I wonder if this dream is a message that when I'm away from them, I'm unsafe or in danger.

So back to the clowns. In that dream, my family and I were walking down a dark street at night. I was on my dad's shoulders, which tells you how young I was. I can't remember whether we were at a fair or not; I just remember that it was kind of busy and definitely dark. I looked to the left and saw some kind of booth. It looked like a giant tent that opened to the street, with a table in the center. In the tent were these evil-looking clowns, probably eight of them. Their eyes were glowing, and there was the scent of sawdust in the air like at a traveling circus.

The clowns were walking around the table like they were conducting a ritual or summoning something powerful. As we walked past, my head was turned as far to the left as it could go. Suddenly the clowns stopped their ritual and stood and stared at me with evil, glowing eyes. Then out of nowhere they started running at me, and no matter how much I screamed, my father wouldn't run away. He continued to walk leisurely as they came closer and closer, no matter how much I begged him to flee. Suddenly I woke up, shaking and terrified. I have had this dream on multiple occasions over the years.

Now fast-forward to today. Every Halloween in Las Vegas, there's this attraction called Fright Dome, which is a haunted house kind of thing that Jason Egan owns and has been running for about ten years now. It has fake animatronic beings and eerie Halloween sounds pumped in, but it's pretty cool, so I decided to go with Aaron and some other friends one year. I mean, for a demon hunter like me who's faced pure evil, there's no real threat, right?

Except there was. One of the haunted houses (I think there are five or more) was circus themed. I didn't think anything of it at the time, but as we rounded a corner I turned to my left to see five demonic-looking clowns standing and staring at me with glowing eyes.

Trigger the panic attack.

I almost dropped to my knees and fainted. This image from my childhood that had scared me to my core was staring me in the face, and I froze. The meaning of the term *déjà vu* hit me like a haymaker punch as something I had lived through in the past came back to me with extreme force. Usually you can't remember where you've seen a déjà vu before; all you really know is that it's familiar. But I knew exactly where I'd seen and felt this moment. The look of the clowns and the glow in their eyes were exactly the same. What they wore, the way they ran at me, the way my head was turned to the left—it was all identical to my dream. It's as if my nightmares growing up had been premonitions of this very moment. It was powerful, and I believe there's some sort of supernatural connection here.

I remember telling the friends I was with that I'd seen this before. (Or I mumbled it—I can't be sure.) Yes, it may have been a coincidence, but I have been to a lot of haunted houses and fairs and had never seen anything so instantly recognizable. I knew beyond a shadow of a doubt that these were the same clowns from my nightmare, and I never knew I could be scared shitless at a haunted Halloween attraction. I mustered up all the strength I had to get myself out of there, and I can tell you right now that I am never going back to Fright Dome.

It's so interesting to me that the people we meet and the things we see, hear, and smell are all shaped by our own consciousness. Ten people can live in the same house but lead ten completely different lives, guided by the conscious that filters their experiences and tells them what's right and wrong, possible and impossible. But I find dreams especially mysterious because we have no control over what we're going to dream about. It's the one time we can't control our conscious, and our subconscious takes over. There are a lot of mysteries to dreams that science can't truly study. It's a fascinating element of human life.

Think about this: How many times have you had a dream about people you want to cross paths with? Or maybe you're with someone in a dream and you wake up feeling sad because you wanted to be with them more and now it's over. Gone. Poof. Maybe the person in the dream is your soul mate or at least someone you'll run into later, like the clowns in my dream. You're interacting with these people and your subconscious is shaping your perceptions of them, but who are they? Are they from your past? Your future? Are they ghosts? Dreams to me are like the paranormal encounters. When you experience them, you question how and why they happened. You awake wanting to know more, but you have a hard time even remembering what happened for more than a few hours afterward. Except for the worst ones, of course.

For me, dreams are an escape, as I expect they are for many people. Life is noisy and busy; you wake up with 5,000 things to do, places to go, and people to see. But in dreams, the physical world doesn't matter. Before I fall asleep, I lie in bed and wonder if the afterlife is like my dreams, where I can think, laugh, and experience emotions like fear and pain and interact with people I've never met.

One day I thought, *I want to have fun with my dreams.* I wanted it to be like *The Matrix,* where I could do what I wanted without consequences. Typically our dreams choose us, not the other way around, but I thought, *What if I took control and did what I wanted in my dreams?* So I trained myself to reverse this power.

I still remember how the dream went. It was just another day in Las Vegas. I looked up, saw myself in bed dreaming, and thought, *Okay, let's go have some fun.* In the dream, I killed people knowing that it wasn't morally wrong. I tricked my mind into doing something totally against its ethical code because I knew it wasn't real. When I think about it, it's kind of disturbing, and now that it's over I don't even like talking about it, but at the time I understood it. I knew I was dreaming and it didn't matter. I've never been able to do it again, and I don't want to.

When I woke up, I knew I had done something bad and freaked out a little. I actually ran to the bathroom to look for the knife I had used to stab everyone to make sure it was still there and not bloody. Was I still dreaming? It was so vivid, yet I knew it wasn't real. I was somewhere between unconsciousness and reality, and it was weird. It was almost like I'd tapped into a world I shouldn't have.

This brings me back to the paranormal. Just like I've tapped into the spirit world on so many occasions, I'd tapped into the dream world, and I didn't know if it would have the same ill effects. Being a paranormal investigator, I've brought evil things home that took me a long time to get rid of. I sincerely hope that's not the case with this dream; I've already got a line of demons to free myself from. But these are the things that keep me going. What's really going on in dreams? How do dreams and the paranormal intertwine? There are so many mysteries in this world that I can't stop thinking about and want to solve. Sometimes I feel like my mind gets obsessed and my body pays the price.

THAT'S NOTHING TO CLOWN ABOUT.

21

APRIL 5

Here's a sad and weird little fact: My two favorite singers died on my birthday. Kurt Cobain of Nirvana and Lane Staley of Alice in Chains both died on April 5. I always listened to them growing up while they were still alive, and no one had any idea that they would end their own lives on my birthday.

It's a strange coincidence, but still, when I'm having a bad day and my mind is a mess, I turn to them. No matter what day it is, what time it is, or how bad of a mood I'm in, I'll listen to two specific songs to pull me out of a funk: "Where Did You Sleep Last Night" by Nirvana and "Nutshell" by Alice in Chains. These songs have so much soul; you can just tell that these two lead singers had so many demons, so much noise in them. These guys were born with unimaginable talent, but when they sing these softer songs, you can connect to the pain and darkness that each of them harbored inside. It was almost as if you could have predicted their deaths.

There's another song by Johnny Cash called "Ain't No Grave" that I listen to a lot. When I made my album, *Necrofusion,* we recorded a song called "Dead Awaiting" that seems to connect with

167

all three of them. "Dead Awaiting" is about the dark thoughts we all have about death and the sadness and fear that come with pondering what will happen when we die. All this great life we know—the smells, sounds, colors, love, happiness, achievements, family, whatever—will stop. The comfort of our consciousness and our selves will be gone, and we don't know what to expect afterward. "Dead Awaiting" is a blend of that fear and the fear of the unknown and the spirits that mark you in this life. The afterlife is a big unknown even for people like me who constantly peek our heads behind the curtain.

I don't ascribe any supernatural meaning to these two singers dying on my birthday, but it is weird that I've been drawn to them and connect with these two songs on a deeper level than any other music out there. Sometimes I'll go on YouTube and watch the live unplugged performances of these songs, and it really connects me to the pain they were going through.

Cobain and Staley were two of the most creative people ever, with minds that never shut down. I like to think of myself as a creative person, and, like theirs, my mind never stops. I can go out and film for a week, but when I come home (depending on how bad the lockdown hangover is), I can be on my phone and computer working hard on the next episode before I even unpack my bags. The creativity never turns off, and I feel that if I don't get on a computer and write down what I'm thinking, then I'll go crazy. I've never been able to sit still, and I think Cobain and Staley were the same way.

But they were also haunted in a way. They had everything—fame, friends, money, attention, people at their beck and call—but it was just noise that added to the overpowering cacophony in their heads and destroyed them in the end. For some creative types, the added attention makes things worse instead of better. They simply can't handle it. Cobain and Staley both killed themselves to end their pain.

I worry about that sometimes, especially when I look at how reclusive I've become. I used to enjoy being around people, but more and more I just want to be left alone and have the freedom to do my job without so many intrusions. Don't be alarmed; I'm not suicidal. But I see myself exhibiting some of the same behavior patterns that they did at times.

One of the great things about being an artist is that you can leave behind a legacy and continue to influence people long after you're gone. Your voice or your art lives on and delivers a powerful message. To this day, "Where Did You Sleep Last Night" has 22 million views and counting on YouTube. I hope that people find meaning in my work and in episodes of *Ghost Adventures* long after I'm gone. I hope that the show helps someone get over their fear of the paranormal or teaches someone to make contact with a loved one. Maybe an episode of *Ghost Adventures* will open the mind of a child to the possibilities of what could be waiting for us when we die and inspire him or her to get into the field and make a breakthrough in paranormal communication.

AND MAYBE THAT EPISODE
WILL AIR ON APRIL 5.

22

OUIJA BOARDS

It takes two to tango.

Ouija boards are old. Since before the turn of the twentieth century, they've been used to conjure up spirits in the comforts of home, which makes the Ouija board the oldest piece of paranormal investigation equipment around and easily the most social. You don't need a haunted location, a professional paranormal investigator, or any special equipment; just grab a friend, light some candles, put your hands on the board, and start freaking out. But Ouija boards have a reputation for being a parlor trick—a reputation that's probably deserved, because they're cheesy and cheap. However, I've seen amazing things happen while people were using them. So should you believe the hype? Stay tuned.

I've investigated cases where Ouija boards were used to conjure up a demon named Zozo. The legend is that Zozo is attached to all Ouija boards and attacks people who use them. During these cases, I worked with Robert Murch, the world's leading expert on Ouija boards, and a man named Darren Evens, who has probably done more research on Zozo than anyone else in the world. In the end, I came away more of a believer in Ouija boards than a skeptic. Surprised? I was too.

The basic concept of a Ouija board is simple: Two people place their hands on a plastic planchette over a board covered in letters, numbers, words, and symbols and ask spirits to join them. The participants open themselves up and ask questions of the spirits, who use the available energy to move the planchette and provide answers. Since its invention, skeptics have called the Ouija board fake and claim that it's an ideomotor response, or involuntary movement by the human participants, rather than real communication with spirits.

My theory is that the Ouija board allows us to tap into a part of ourselves that we still don't understand. This world is complicated and mysterious, and if scientists can't tell us how the energies and consciousness within their own bodies work, then how can they tell us that our subconscious is moving a planchette while we're awake? Can some of the planchette movement be caused by an ideomotor response? Sure, but that response is a subconscious event, and there's evidence that suggests spirit connections take place in the subconscious. So it could be that a spirit is using the person's subconscious to move the planchette, and we just call it an ideomotor response because we have a need to explain everything.

We don't fully know how our brains work yet, but there's definitely more that we don't know than we do know. We don't use 100 percent of our brains, so there's a portion that's virtually untapped, and just waiting for the right moment to be activated. I believe that part of the brain can help us do great things, and maybe it can be accessed by using a Ouija board. I know that using one can open up a portal and call upon spirits because I've seen it happen.

The thing about a Ouija board is that you need two people to make it work, with both people focusing their energies on the planchette. A Ouija board forces you to concentrate on a single point. I believe that when two people are doing that in harmony and you ask a spirit to speak, you're opening up a new part of your mind and body. You're exercising and strengthening your mind to open up to an interaction with a ghost.

I believe that a lot of mysteries within ourselves can be uncovered during a Ouija board session. You're constantly asking your partner if he moved the planchette, and he's thinking you did it, but the whole time it's really energy from a part of your body that you never use that is contacting a nearby spirit. The average person who doesn't have a constant spirit attachment might be afraid or nervous, which can affect the outcome. But when two people believe in something strongly enough, then it becomes emotional, and emotions can unlock connections to spirits and invite them into our lives through the Ouija board.

Some people say that there's no difference between a Ouija board and a K2 meter or a digital recorder that's used to capture EVPs, but that's BS, and I'll tell you why. When you use a K2 meter or digital recorder, you're just asking a question. You're not as focused as two people concentrating on a single point would be, and you're not tapping into the natural energies of two people to get a spirit to come through (and they do). Not everyone is a paranormal investigator, but it's easy to have a paranormal encounter with a Ouija board because you and your partner are contributing different energies. It's a memorable experience, but it has a dark side that everyone should be aware of.

In a case we investigated in Oklahoma, a man had used a Ouija board and conjured up the Zozo demon. Those who call upon Zozo frequently see the planchette on the Ouija board go back forth between the Z and O over and over again: Z-O-Z-O-Z-O-Z-O-Z-O. Zozo has been known to attack and sexually assault people when summoned, and I believe he waits for people to get their minds and focus into the red zone on the emotional tachometer before he comes through. There have been numerous credible

These things are more dangerous than you think.

cases of Zozo coming through Ouija board sessions, so it's more than a myth to me.

Zozo could be the spirit of a man named Walter Kenilworth, a palm reader in the early twentieth century who claimed that he stole people's souls through his readings. Kenilworth published books on how he used his psychic powers to steal souls and money, so there's a theory that Kenilworth is Zozo and comes through Ouija boards to attack people.

Darren Evens is one of those people. He has not only summoned Zozo, but may also have a personal connection to it. Darren has done a lot of research on Zozo, and Zozo actually came through during a Ouija board session. Zozo picked up Darren's daughter and threw her down the stairs, which obviously hurt her and scared him. After spending time with Darren, I believe that Zozo is part of him, but he doesn't know it.

We went to Darren's house to film an episode of *Ghost Adventures,* and we had some bizarre experiences there. Our tech, Jay Wasley, was with us during this session. Jay also has a connection to Zozo and was almost killed by it once. During an earlier Ouija board session, a friend of Jay's was overcome by the demon and suddenly jumped on top of Jay and tried to stab him. To this day, the Ouija board makes Jay uncomfortable, but we convinced him to take another "stab" at it for this episode and participate in a session with Darren. Of course, crazy things happened, and I'm convinced that Zozo came through.

The session we did in Oklahoma was with a group of people who know the Ouija Board well. We've all had experiences with it and are deep into the paranormal, with histories of attachments and sensitive abilities. In addition to that, we were in a house that had a lot of paranormal residue from Darren's previous sessions. So there was quite a bit of paranormal energy there, and I believe our spirit attachments fought with each other for control when we were trying to contact Zozo. At one point, Darren's wife left the house and came back with her pants unbuttoned and belt undone, saying that Zozo had sexually attacked her. We also caught a lot of noises and other evidence during the session that remain unexplained.

Whatever the truth is, my eyes have been opened to the dangers of Ouija boards. The weird thing is that you can buy them at Toys "R" Us. Is there more to this company that we don't know? I'd love to talk to them and see if they realize the harm these boards can cause. We won't send a kid into space, but we'll give him a portal to another dimension and invite a demon in. It makes me wonder if Walter Kenilworth's descendants are shareholders and the whole thing is just a big ploy to make money.

IT WOULDN'T SURPRISE ME.

23

LOCKDOWN
HANGOVER

It's way worse than
a regular one.

Just about everyone has experienced a hangover. You go out, you have fun, you drink too much, and the next day you wake up in pain and make a list of the people you need to apologize to. The day after a lockdown is no different…except for the lack of booze.

I've evolved as an investigator, and as time goes by I release more and more of myself to the spirits I come in contact with. I let them use my body however they need to, opening the door to the spirit world wider and wider. This has resulted in deeper and deeper connections, but it comes at a price. The more I allow spirits in, the more sensitive I become to them and the more damage they can do, even long after a lockdown is over. Early on, when I had only a few investigations under my belt, I learned how important it is to trust what your body is telling you. Some of us are like tuning forks or lightning rods for the paranormal, but like anyone who abuses his body in any way, I start feeling the consequences of that abuse over time.

I'm very much in tune with myself. I can recognize a skipped heartbeat, a wheeze in the lungs, a sudden attack of goosebumps, or a powerful wave of sorrow, and I know what they all mean during a paranormal environment. I don't do this once in a while as a hobby in my free time; I do it all the time for a living. I'm frequently on an emotional, empathetic level with spirits, and I'm sure they know that I'm in tune with their world. It's almost like a part of me has already passed over, and the spirits can sense that and reach out to me as a result. I truly believe that I'm connected to the afterlife in some small way, but it's taken its toll on me. After a lockdown I'm always in pain, and some lockdowns are worse than others.

Our investigation of the Sorrel Weed House in Savannah, Georgia, gave me a three-alarm hangover. It was very similar to a real one—headache, nausea, dizziness, throbbing, memory loss—but weirder. I can usually gauge how bad my hangover is going to be by the interactions I have with spirits during a lockdown, but this one threw me for a loop. It was an incredible connection, sure, but the lasting impression it left on me was disproportionately huge.

At the house, I came into contact with a powerful spirit in the slave quarters that I'll never forget. This spirit wasn't just strong; it reached inside me and let me feel its emotions, connecting us like a cross-dimensional umbilical cord. Moments like this are always strange and unpredictable, but I've long since thrown caution to the wind, so I opened myself up and allowed it in. What did I get for that? I was paralyzed. I stood motionless and frozen in time, unaware of my surroundings for several moments. You lose all sense of time and space when a spirit takes a hold of you like that. You don't recognize the people around you. You don't know what time it is. Nothing is familiar, and your head swims until you fall into a trancelike state.

It's this moment, when the spirit is drawing your energy from you and you are feeling the spirit's emotions, that really drains your body. There's a scene in *Bram Stoker's Dracula* where Keanu Reeves' character is being held hostage by female vampires. They continuously suck his blood, but they leave a tiny bit so he's barely alive. That's exactly what a lockdown hangover feels like. That's how deep I get into these experiences. These hangovers are the worst because it can take days to get my body working properly again.

I love these intimate interactions and ethereal moments with spirits, but the next day kicks me in the gut. It took me five days to get over that investigation in Savannah. I was nauseated, dizzy, and just plain off. And it shook me up not only because it took me so long to get over it, but also because I was so irritated with everyone afterward. We all go our separate ways the day after a lockdown, and I usually ride to the airport with Billy and Aaron. This is when we're most on edge with each other because the residue of an evil spirit takes time to wear off. When we have an emotional moment during a spirit interaction, channeling, or possession, we end up carrying the residue of that spirit, and it takes a little while to get ourselves back to normal.

We know this now and have learned to stay quiet until we're home because no one wants to say something he'll regret. We even keep the joking to a minimum. We can turn on a dime, and we usually try to talk as little as possible so we don't. On the way home from Savannah, though, Billy and I got into it because my connection with the spirit stuck with me and changed me for a while. But in the end, it was worth it to me. I'm convinced that the longer and stronger the hangover, the deeper the connection was with the spirit.

My lockdown hangovers make me wonder what these interactions might be doing to me. Spirit interaction is like a drug that you develop a dependency on. Addicts return to their "precious" no matter how severe the effects, and in some ways I guess I'm no different. The rush is not without its consequences. I've developed a lot of health issues from the locations I've investigated. In addition to respiratory troubles, I believe I've developed other, deeper problems from opening myself up to spirits. These lockdown hangovers seem to take more and more of a beating on me. They get harder and harder and take longer and longer to get over. This is my career and my passion, but at what point do I say, "It's not worth it anymore"? Professional athletes all go through this, and though I was never destined to play in the NFL, I have something in common with those men who lead a life that physically destroys them. I have to be realistic and figure out when it's time to step away and do something else. And that makes me sad.

The lockdown hangover cure is more than just carrying a crystal in your pocket, saying a prayer, or burning some sage. Those types of cures can help a little, but they're more mental than anything—placebos, really. The only real way to flush out a lockdown hangover is to get home and work it out. I like to go to Red Rock Canyon near Las Vegas and let nature cleanse me. It's a spiritual place that was once home to the Paiute Indians, and I feel that being there rids me of any negative crap I bring home. I don't really do anything out there; I just stare off into the distance and ask Mother Nature to help me out. It keeps me from going insane sometimes. That and my dog, Gracie.

Gracie has always been there for me, and I'm lucky to have her. I occasionally do work for the Nevada Society for the Prevention of Cruelty to Animals (NSPCA), and one day I went to a shelter and one of the workers said to me, "I think you need to meet somebody." Suddenly this dog ran toward me from about 40 feet away and gave me the biggest hug ever, like we were old friends and she was glad to see me after a long separation. I immediately felt this energy and power, like she was there for a reason. She's a pure soul, and I really believe that Gracie was sent to me by a higher power to help get me through tough times. Between her, the canyons, and Mother Nature, the lockdown hangovers don't stand a chance.

THEY STILL SUCK, BUT I ALWAYS FIND A WAY TO BEAT THEM.

Gracie loves hiking at Red Rock Canyon.

24

POST-POSSESSION BLUES

It's a state of mind.

I got a question on Twitter one day: "What does it feel like after a possession?" The short answer is that I feel confused. It might be a horrible analogy, but the best thing I can compare it to is being drugged. Being possessed is like being out of control and not wanting to be. I would compare it to coming out of anesthesia (see chapter 19, "Overland Hotel," on my nasal surgery for the painful details of that ride), but it's not quite the same.

A possession is unexpected. You lose control of your body, which really sucks. You fight it, but no matter how badly you want the evil spirit gone, it persists until it's ready to leave on its own or is forced out by an exorcism. You want to regain your consciousness and retake control of your body, mind, and feelings because, trust me, you're not the one calling the shots in those situations. You know that something bad has entered your system, and while it's rooting around in your house, the things you see with your eyes are foreign to you. The world you know (or thought you knew) looks and feels totally different. You don't recognize people. Your personality is no longer yours. The most noticeable part is that others who know you look at you and know that it isn't you. Everyone stares and asks if you're okay, like you're having a serious freak medical problem.

My worst possessions to date occurred at Poveglia Island in Italy and my return to Bobby Mackey's Music World in Kentucky. At both locations I encountered something strong that got in and took over my body and mind and took a long time to get rid of. They were both painful experiences, but what I felt invade my soul at the Demon House that I own in Indiana was frightfully powerful (see chapter 3 for more on that). I am not keen on the idea of it happening again. That place is evil, and I will have to take massive precautions before I return.

A possession feels like you're driving down the road with your family and someone tries to grab the wheel and steer you into a tree and kill everyone. But they're using your hands and you can't understand what's happening. You feel like a puppet of the devil, and when the demon leaves and you regain control of yourself, you feel very strange.

You also feel confused and ask yourself a lot of questions. *Why did it happen to me and no one else? What did the demon want? Did it cause permanent damage? Am I going to hell now? How do I make sure I'm clean? How do I keep it from happening again?* All these thoughts fly around in your head, and it takes some people a long time to clear them away and rediscover who they are. A possession can really shake your faith and make you doubt yourself.

The body's reaction to a possession is indescribable. Some people don't remember anything about the experience; there are moments I don't recall even when I see them replayed on film. That's truly surreal and scary. At other times I was aware of what was going on, but I was just a passenger on a vehicle I couldn't control. I was outside my body watching the events go down, and there was nothing I could do about it but fight to get my body back. Regaining control is a little like being stuck in a nightmare and fighting your way out of it to wake up. It's the definition of weird.

After my possession at Bobby Mackey's, the residual effects stayed with me for months, but at the exact moment I felt the demon leave my body, there was instant relief, and I just wanted to sleep. I was a puppet, and the puppeteer had cut the strings. My energy sapped, my legs gave out, and I nearly collapsed.

Is there a sick part of me that enjoys it? Yes. Because when you're possessed, time stands still. Nothing matters. You don't think about your problems or your pain or the world you're used to. All the things that make me who I am are gone. That release of self and seeing the world through different filters is a bit of a rush. In no way am I saying that a possession is fun, and I spend every minute of it trying to break free, but my mind doesn't work like everyone else's. I've explored the worst holes on Earth and seem to find beauty and wonder in walking paths that most people disregard as disgusting. Spirits have opened my mind, like a musician with a muse that helps him write better music. They've made me a better investigator by repeatedly exposing me to death and the afterlife.

Have you ever had a dream where you did something very bad but secretly enjoyed it a little? I mean a vivid dream in which you are conscious of this bad thing you're doing, and when you wake up you get a little thrill from the bad thing you did. You shake it off and think, *Oh my God. Why did I just enjoy that a little?* When I was possessed, everything in me was bad, but I didn't really care. A part of me even liked it, but that part wasn't me. You don't accept it, but a part of you wants to, and reconciling those two sides is tough.

During a possession, I have one singular goal: to not be possessed anymore. Maybe what I secretly enjoy, then, is the fight. The struggle against dark forces reinforces my belief that good can prevail in the end. Maybe I like knowing that I truly can make contact with the other side—that even though it's a dark entity trying to take over, at least it chose me, and I'm still bridging the divide between this world and the next.

I can sit in a chair all day and revisit places I've already been and be entertained by the spirits that are still there and call to me. Unlike the guy in the Dos Equis commercials, I'm not the most interesting man in the world, but I feel that I live in a more interesting place than most. It's not made up only of material things and present-day society. Money, women, houses, cars...those aren't the things I live for. The more places I investigate, the more spirits I come in contact with, and the more possessions I endure, the more I can just sit and reflect on those experiences and ask myself billions of questions about life and death and how it all works.

Going through a possession doesn't mean that you're screwed for life. The boy on whom *The Exorcist* was based went on to lead a successful life long after the demon was cast out of him. Dr. William Bradshaw, one of the most successful and knowledgeable demonologists in the world, believes that demons choose their victims at an early age. They prefer people with great potential who will have an impact on the world, but why? Why do they choose to possess people who are gifted or are destined to do something great? And does this mean that our fate is determined before we're even born? Have great people been marked from birth? Is there really no free will, and are those who say that God has a plan for everyone correct? Can you see how a seemingly insignificant thing like a possession can lead me to ask the biggest questions in the universe?

Sometimes I feel that a possession can do a person good. While it's hell to go through (literally), the people who experience a possession go on to live great lives with no recollection of the event. Maybe it makes them stronger in the end, like any traumatic event can make a person more resilient. No one knows what demons are. No one has been able to study or dissect one. I'm not taking the side of demons—I do think they're evil—but I'm not comfortable making blanket statements about something so difficult to study. Demons make you feel evil, make you want to do violent things, and make you say horrible things. They are nasty and can cause you harm.

But when a demon possesses you, does it really do damage to your body, or does it actually help it? Can a dose of supernatural energy that makes you levitate, speak in Latin, or have superhuman strength make you a better person in the long run? Think about it—a godlike power is entering your body and giving you its power. When it leaves, what does it leave behind? You won't know what effects it had until years later. Does a spirit entering your body energize your organs or cells? Does it prevent disease? Do demons get diseased? Do they die?

So MANY QUESTIONS AND SO FEW ANSWERS.

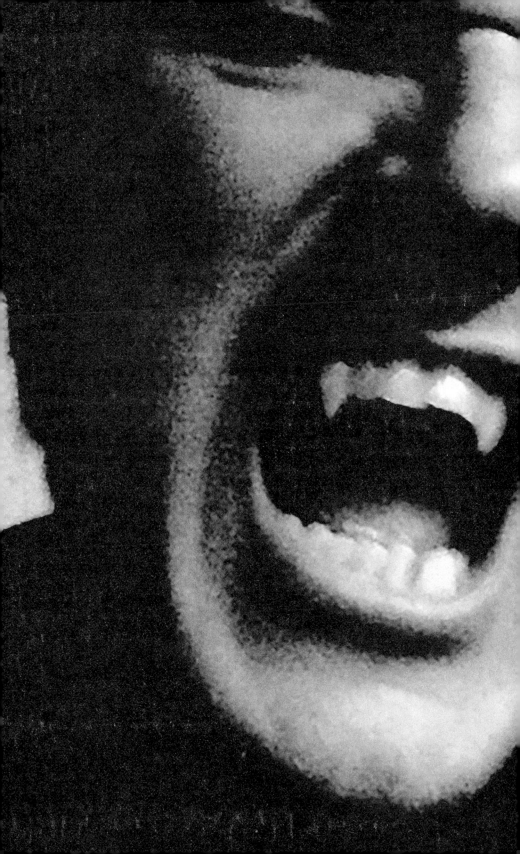

25

TRANS-ALLEGHENY LUNATIC ASYLUM

What you don't know can hurt you.

When we came up with the concept to do a live paranormal investigation at the Trans-Allegheny Lunatic Asylum on Halloween night, there were a ton of obstacles for us to overcome. How could we examine evidence quickly and thoroughly on the spot? How could we broadcast a live event without the equipment and people getting in the way (because a live event would certainly involve a larger crew)? Could we really sustain a seven-hour event? Was there any place for Aaron to eat in Weston, West Virginia? How many times would Aaron fart on live TV? How would I edit that out? A lot of the variables that are under my control in a regular lockdown would be uncontrollable in a live event, so it was going to take some creative thinking to pull it off.

I saw this as a challenge and took it on as a mission, but my biggest worry was getting a migraine. At the time I was suffering from massive migraines that would last for one to two days and would be triggered by any number of crazy things. A migraine would really slow me down, so I was worried that one would kick in at the exact wrong moment. Four days before the event, we arrived in Weston to get ready for the show, and I remember worrying every day: When will the migraine kick in? At the time they were so bad that I knew I wouldn't be myself if I got one. I wouldn't be able to think clearly and talk right. This was a seven-hour live event with millions of people watching, and I had to not just lead it, but make it meaningful and memorable. Doing that would be impossible with a migraine, so the pressure to avoid one was absolutely massive.

We did research and walk-throughs and set up a ton of equipment—I think we had forty remote camera operators and six production trucks. It was like NASA, and I was Snake Pliskin in *Escape from New York*. The pressure was on, and I knew that if I got a migraine, I would be in a fog and wouldn't be able to speak or work. I wouldn't be myself. I live in Vegas and see people do live shows on the Strip every night, and I think they must be in perfect health to perform so often.

During the investigation I wore an earpiece the whole time, with our award-winning producer Bruce Kennedy on the other end. Bruce is amazing to work with, and he kept me on a strict time line by telling me when to wrap up a particular segment, when to go to commercial, when to go to the front door of the asylum to bring in new guests, when to go to Dave at the nerve center to talk about new evidence, when any problems arose, etc. All this while leading a live paranormal investigation and maintaining our credibility. I'd never done live TV before, so to jump into it for the first time with a seven-hour show, with several more hours of interviews afterward, was a huge accomplishment for me, Nick, Aaron, the production staff, and everyone else involved.

Except for one.

I wanted to bring in guest investigators for an hour each to add to the experience. We brought in Mark and Debby Constantino, who are awesome investigators and EVP specialists. We also brought in one of the leading psychic mediums, Chris Fleming, and some fans, including Kelly Crigger, who helped me write this book and my previous one, *Dark World.* Kelly got locked in a seclusion cell at the asylum and heard the creepiest disembodied scream ever.

Around the fourth or fifth hour, we brought in Robert Bess, whom I'd never met. I'd investigated with the Constantinos and Chris Fleming, and they always do amazing work (and got amazing results that night at the asylum). But the first time I met Robert Bess was the moment I met him live on camera. For some reason we had never crossed paths during the preparation for the show, so I was meeting him in front of millions of people. It was risky (especially because the stress of the unknown could trigger a migraine), but I figured it was worth the risk because he brought a new piece of technology to the show, and from what I had heard, it got results. Looking back on that night, it wasn't the best idea.

I think it was Dave Schrader who told me about Bess and his Parabot device: a chamber large enough to hold a human, flanked by large electric Tesla coils. It is supposed to be able to attract and contain the electromagnetic energy created by spirits. Dave sent me a video of the device in action, and it looked really interesting. It looked and sounded like something from *Ghostbusters,* but it came from a credible source, so I said yes, let's bring him on the live show. I love experimenting with new technologies and techniques, and this thing was pretty captivating. Could it really capture and hold a spirit?

A few days before the live show, the production crew had a couple of incidents with the Parabot that they told me about. While it was sitting in a hallway of the Trans-Allegheny Lunatic Asylum, the glass on the inside of the device cracked. Bess explained this as angry ghosts that didn't like the device and were trying to sabotage it. I actually got to step inside the Parabot and see the cracks. Another day the fluorescent lights above the Parabot came crashing down on it unexplainably. So I was really amped to get this thing on the show and work with Bess.

I met Bess on set (decked out in his cowboy hat and long leather coat) in the middle of the night in front of the world. He fired up the device, and I was immediately concerned about the sheer amperage coming off of it. It was like he was trying to resuscitate Frankenstein's monster with massive jolts of electricity. The Parabot made a sound every few seconds—*boom boom boom*—and I could feel the shock waves in the air every time it fired. Clearly it had power. It was like the human version of a bug zapper, and I was waiting for one of us to get electrocuted. I seriously thought one of us was going to get killed by the thing, especially when Bess said to me, "Don't get within three feet of it." Getting incinerated on live TV would not be good.

But while this thing was pumping out electricity, I could feel the environment change. The air was supercharged, and since spirits are thought to be made of electromagnetic energy, I thought maybe this was a great invention and we were going to see some results. Bess said that when the door opened, the ghosts would go toward the energy, and he would capture them in the pod by closing the door. I thought, *Okay. Let me see this.*

So we let Bess do his thing, and I will say that legitimately strange things started happening. Nick said that he felt something grabbing his leg, so I took a still shot of his legs and captured a huge white anomaly. It was like a spirit was being dragged toward the Parabot and was grabbing Nick's leg to avoid being sucked in. Then I took another picture down the hallway we were in and captured a green manifestation moving toward the Parabot. Aaron started freaking out because he was standing close to the coils and felt like the device was messing with him internally, so I pushed him back and told him to keep his distance, because none of us knew what the side effects of this thing were. It was an experiment, and we all know how horribly wrong an experiment can go and how quickly it can turn.

I was feeling pretty good about the Parabot and Bess when it all went bad. Something hit the floor, and it was loud—loud enough to make Nick, Aaron, and me jump. I had no idea that the EMF detector that was in Bess' hand had left his hand, hit the floor, and slid down the hallway. All I knew was that something had hit the ground, and we all reacted.

It wasn't until after we had finished with Bess and the Parabot and moved on to the final hour of the show to investigate an abandoned hospital that we got the bad news from the guys back at the nerve center: It appeared that Robert Bess had thrown the device. "Hey, Zak, listen, man," Bruce said in my earpiece. "We reviewed the X-cam footage, the night vision footage, and the static footage from the robotic camera, and it really looks like the EMF detector was thrown."

No way, I thought. We were almost across the finish line, and this news stopped me in my tracks. Then Dave Schrader's voice came across my earpiece: "Yeah, this looks really convincing that he threw it." They asked if I wanted Dave to say something to the audience from the nerve center, and I agreed. I told them to have Dave word it in a way that made it seem suspect, and to suggest that it was not paranormal. Dave delivered the perfect NFL analogy when he said, "Was this intentional grounding?"

They then asked if I wanted to confront Bess about the incident. "Hell yes," I said. Unfortunately, that meant cutting the last investigation short, because we were on live TV and had a time limit, but it was worth it to resolve the issue. We planned a final goodbye on camera with all of our guests, like Pat Sajak does on *Wheel of Fortune,* but they gave me an extra three minutes to confront Bess afterward. It was going to be uncomfortable, but my reputation—and that of everyone else who had worked on the show—was on the line. It had to be done publicly and immediately. I knew it was important to send a message to everyone that we have high standards for our investigations. I never condone behavior like that, and since I was in charge of the investigation, it was my responsibility to say something about it on the spot.

At the end of the show, I was interviewed by the host, Dean Haglund (the dude from *The X-Files*), and then I went up to Bess and asked him face-to-face what had happened. I told him that I hadn't seen the video, but everyone was telling me that it looked like he had thrown the EMF detector. He denied it, but days later, when I reviewed the evidence, it seemed pretty clear that he had thrown the device.

This pissed me off back then and still pisses me off to this day. Robert Bess tarnished what was otherwise a great investigation. Forget that it was a live TV show and the production crew and Travel Channel executives were there; we brought Bess into our crew to do paranormal research, and he violated our trust, which disrespected us and everything we had worked for. It was disappointing, because so many people worked so hard to make it a great event, and everything else had gone off without a hitch.

I take personal responsibility for bringing Bess on the show and therefore anything he did as our guest, so as soon as I saw the video and knew that he'd thrown it, I was upset with myself. Even though 95 percent of the show went perfectly, I still felt like I'd let everyone down, but I also believe that I did the right thing in calling him out. If I hadn't, then it would have made *Ghost*

Adventures a party to the crime. In the end we turned a negative into a positive.

THAT'S WHEN THE MIGRAINE FINALLY HIT.

26
LOCATION DISAPPOINTMENTS

Not every "haunted" place turns out to be a paranormal hotspot.

I hate letdowns, but some of the locations we investigate just don't turn up any good evidence. Keep in mind that just because we don't turn up any evidence during our investigation doesn't mean that the place isn't haunted or that there's no activity there; it just means that we weren't able to capture any on that particular night. Still, I consider it a personal failure, because it's my job to entice the spirits to make contact with us. It's my role to research what happened at a location and find out what makes the spirits trapped there want to be heard or seen, and then use that knowledge to bring them out. Otherwise I'm just a chump walking around in the dark asking silly questions.

The most disappointing location we've filmed for *Ghost Adventures* was probably the Gribble House Warehouse in Savannah, Georgia. The Excalibur nightclub in Chicago and the jail at Cripple Creek in Colorado were also disappointments, but the Gribble House Warehouse was the pits. There's a fine line between a truly haunted location and a location that's being sensationalized by a tour company, and I got a lesson in the two on that trip.

Now, I'm not saying for certain that this is the case at the Gribble House, but there was something fishy going on down south. A local tour company was touting the location as the "Gribble House Paranormal Experience," which should have raised red flags in my mind. I'm not against companies teaching the public how to ghost hunt and leading them into certain areas to give them a true paranormal experience—I'm all for it, in fact, so I can't speak negatively about the practice. But I do think it's being sensationalized there.

The real Gribble House is gone. It was a private residence that was built in the early twentieth century, and three women were murdered there in 1909. The house was torn down in 1940, and now there's just a warehouse where the Gribble House used to sit. It's new and clean and didn't feel anything like the places I'm used to investigating. Where the Gribble House once stood, supplies are now stored, and to me it felt like I was walking around a Sam's Club. There are walls within the warehouse that separate a storage area, and the tour operator says that area is about the same square footage as the old Gribble House and claims that the company has detected a lot of paranormal activity there. Sorry, but I don't buy it.

I think land has something to do with paranormal activity, but structures play a larger role in hauntings—walls, floors, ceilings, bricks, and mortar store more paranormal energy than the land itself does. Sacred Indian lands, burial grounds, mines, and tunnels can hold onto spiritual energy, but an open field where a house once stood is hard to believe as paranormal. Think about the Stone Tape Theory, which says that certain natural materials can store supercharged emotional events and play them back like a cassette tape under the right conditions (more on that in chapter 14, "Carrying Spirits").

The Gribble House is gone, so none of the materials that were present during the murders are there anymore. Where the house once stood is just a spot in a warehouse. When we were there doing interviews, I felt like the people who lived and worked there were hamming it up for the cameras and their own tour group. It's an interesting story, and I give them mad props for telling the tale of what happened there, but as far as hauntings go, I was not convinced then and am not convinced now.

During the Gribble House tour, people are given information that I believe feeds into their psyche and leads them to think that paranormal events are happening when they're not. They're told things like, "People in this room feel their neck being squeezed," and, "Over here where the house was, we hear women screaming, and over here where the slave quarters were, African Americans feel uncomfortable." When the tourists (who are not professional paranormal investigators) are told these things during a haunted tour they are taking to get a spook or a thrill, they're going to experience those things whether they really happen or not. They're being programmed to hear or feel them, and they think they do. It's Mentalism 101.

When I was filming an episode of *Paranormal Challenge,* we did an experiment with the publisher of *Skeptic* magazine (who is not a believer...shocking). He took a couple of groups on the show around the Linda Vista Hospital and gave them different pieces of false information in the same rooms. He told the first group that in a particular room there was a spirit of an old man that liked to poke people in the head, and told another group that in the same room a young girl had died and would put her hand in your hand. Sure enough, someone in the first group felt a poke in the head, even though that "evidence" was patently false. It's one way to show how the mind can be tricked or even programmed.

The Gribble House warehouse felt like this to me, and though it's not necessarily fraudulent, it's specious at best. Telling the story of what happened there in a fantastical way just establishes the conditions for people to have the experience you want them to have. That's why professional paranormal investigators have to go into a location with a completely open mind and no preconceived notions. This isn't the same as not doing research, though. We always research our locations, but we don't let the research fool us into thinking that we've captured something paranormal when we really haven't.

THAT WOULD RUIN OUR CREDIBILITY, WHICH IS A CRITICAL PART OF OUR STANDING IN THIS FIELD.

27

DEBUNKING

If you don't do it right,
then you're just a scam artist.

Paranormal investigators are a lot more skeptical than you might think, but we focus our skepticism on ourselves rather than on the ghosts. We know they're there, but that doesn't mean every little bump in the night is paranormal unless it's been thoroughly debunked and there is no other possible conclusion. *Debunking* is the act of proving something false, and it's a critical part of every paranormal investigation. To be considered a professional paranormal investigator, you have to go the extra mile to debunk what may or may not be a piece of paranormal evidence. There's so much skepticism surrounding the paranormal that every possible measure has to be taken to remove as many variables as possible and ensure the integrity of the evidence.

The measure of any good investigator is not only how he investigates the unknown, but also how he explains the explainable. You have to be willing to take the time to prove that a weird event could be totally natural. Being able to do that shapes you into a good paranormal investigator and strengthens your evidence. When a door slams or you hear a voice or see an apparition, you can't just assume that it's paranormal. Debunking means asking the hard questions: Where could the sound or vision have come from? Is there anything else it could be? And a hundred more questions, until there's no doubt in your mind that it's truly paranormal.

Frequently, new teams we meet present us with evidence they've captured, but I never assume that it's paranormal until I've thoroughly examined it myself. While investigating Thornhaven Manor in Indiana, for example, we met a GAC-affiliated team who were certain they'd captured the voice of a woman screaming on a digital recorder. It definitely sounded like a woman screaming for her life. But after these folks left, and before we started filming, I decided to investigate this scream. I sent Nick inside the house with a camera, and I stayed outside to determine whether we could find any kind of contamination to explain the recurring sound. A lot of famous haunted locations have this kind of phenomenon: a recurring event like a woman in white walking along a balcony that attracts visitors, but is really just reflection of light. I wanted to make sure that this wasn't the case at Thornhaven Manor. And my hunch was right.

As I stood outside, a neighbor drove his old car past the house, and sure enough, as he stepped on the brakes, it made a screeching sound that sounded exactly like what I'd heard on the digital recorder. Immediately Nick called me on the radio and said that he'd heard a woman scream inside the house. I was like, "I think this is debunked, brother." And it was. Jay Wasley replayed the audio of both events and compare the waveforms, and they matched. There was no doubt that the scream was actually the neighbor's car brakes, which we presented to the owner of the house and the team. Don't get me wrong...this is a good team that does great work, but this one piece of evidence wasn't debunked properly.

FUN FACT:

WHILE FILMING *PARANORMAL CHALLENGE*, I WORKED WITH THE BEST PARANORMAL EXPERTS, AND WE CAME UP WITH HIGH STANDARDS FOR DEBUNKING EVIDENCE. TEAMS WHO DEBUNKED PROPERLY SCORED MORE POINTS WITH THE JUDGES, BECAUSE DEBUNKING IS OFTEN MORE IMPORTANT THAN CAPTURING EVIDENCE.

Titles like "Most Haunted Home in America" always raise a red flag for me. People who come up with titles like this, or with lists of the most haunted locations, often take evidence into account that hasn't been debunked. So the claims of "most haunted" are usually exaggerated, because a lot of the events that people capture there are actually explainable. I'm okay with calling a place "super-duper haunted" if it really is—like if it has verified deaths or legitimate demon attacks associated with it—but I get irritated with places that lure tourists by bragging about how haunted they are when they really just have squeaky floors and loose air vents.

The Whaley House in San Diego is legitimately haunted, but we were able to debunk a big part of it when we did our investigation there. In the 1850s, Thomas Whaley built the house on the site of a gallows where a lot of people were hanged, including a man named Yankee Jim Robinson. Whaley probably cursed himself by putting his house there, but people do strange things. It's said that the house is haunted by Yankee Jim and others killed on the site, but there's more. Whaley's daughter committed suicide in the house, and there have been documented instances of police officers being strangled by unseen forces in the house. Many of the hauntings that the Whaleys experienced were documented, and there are a lot of reports of dark energy, so all the necessary elements were in place for a great investigation.

We heard a lot of reports about a woman crying on the main staircase, so we focused our attention there one night. We were setting up a laser microphone experiment with Bill Chappell when Nick stepped on a stair, and we all heard the sound of a woman singing or crying. But then it happened again when Nick stepped on the same stair, which made me think that it wasn't paranormal. After following the boards through the wall and down the hall, we discovered a domino effect—one board would rub against another and make the sound. It wasn't paranormal at all. It was just a loose board that was connected to another loose board, and when pressure was applied to it (like Nick stepping on it), it made a strange noise that could easily be mistaken for a woman's voice. Debunked!

To gain and maintain credibility and respect, you have to dismiss false positives at every opportunity. The worst part of not debunking information is that it can build up and become an urban legend. If one person or team doesn't debunk an event, then the next team goes in looking for that particular event to happen, and it snowballs. Eventually you end up creating a ghost where there isn't one—or worse, a ghost that becomes false history. That does a disservice to the location and the people who lived or work there. Paranormal investigators should preserve the integrity of a haunted location, not desecrate it.

I'm always asked why we investigate at night. "Don't ghosts come out during the day, Zak?" Of course they do, but our chances of catching them are a lot higher at night. One of the biggest reasons we investigate at night is that the world is a quieter place after dark. There's less possibility of noise contamination from cars, humans, animals, technology, unicorns in heat, whatever. Light contamination is also a problem during the day because the sun casts shadows that can be mistaken for spirits (or basic movement) when there aren't any present. And special equipment like infrared and full-spectrum cameras that frequently capture ethereal events like mists and apparitions don't work as well during the day. So there are plenty of reasons why paranormal investigators are nocturnal creatures.

We were investigating a haunted bed-and-breakfast in Charleston, South Carolina, and showed a third-party investigator why we work at night. We did an investigation during the day equipped with a full-spectrum camera and a regular camera, and it was easy to see the shadows wreaking havoc all over the film. They were everywhere, and the sunlight caused many different visual distortions in videos and digital still photos. The background noise levels were much higher, too, so just getting a basic EVP was a chore.

But the biggest reason we work at night is so that we can use infrared light. If you know anything about the light spectrum, you know that the amount of light humans can see with the naked eye

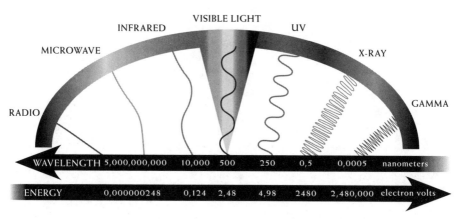

is very small. We can't see ultraviolet or infrared light, but since we're smarter than the average ape, we've developed the technology to help us see beyond what is normally visible to us.

Why is this important? Many people (myself included) feel that spirits reside in the infrared and/or ultraviolet spectrum, or at least can be illuminated by these forms of light. Night vision cameras shoot in infrared and amplify existing ambient light, so they have the capability to see things we can't see with the naked eye. I believe that infrared light can illuminate a ghost's composition—an orb, a mist, a vapor, or an ectoplasm—under the right conditions, so I use this equipment often. I've thoroughly investigated the Portland underground, which is an active place during the day, but it's not the same as working at night. Like people, the paranormal activity down there is vastly different after the sun goes down.

AND ALL OF IT HAS TO BE DEBUNKED.

28

GUEST
INVESTIGATORS

Some are great.
Others are just distractions.

The Ghost Adventures Crew has been doing this job long enough now that we can literally calibrate our energies and connect without speaking. We can all sense when something paranormal is happening to someone else. We've been in many dire and scary situations, and we know that each of us is solid; we have each other's backs. But sometimes it's good to throw an unknown entity into the mix to see what happens.

We got the idea to bring in guest investigators for a short period to give *Ghost Adventures* a different energy and offer the viewers a new outlook on the location. Sometimes the guest's energy adds to ours to improve the experience, but it isn't always harmonious. Some of the celebrity investigators we've had on the show were not the easiest people to work with.

In this field, you have to work with people you know and trust and who take the operation seriously. I like to work with people who are sensitive to paranormal energy or have some other sort of gift or value to bring to the table. The more I've grown in this field, the more I enjoy not having celebrity investigators anymore. More often than not, they're a distraction that throws off our energy. Either they've never done this sort of thing, or they think you have to put on a show for them and bring out unbelievable ghosts to entertain them. I don't need that kind of pressure when I investigate.

However, I do have a couple of favorites among the guest investigators we've had on the show. UFC heavyweight contender Brendan Schaub is a genuine person whom I met during a pet rescue charity event at the Stanley Hotel outside of Denver. I've been a UFC fan for a long time, so it was great to meet him, and we became friends afterward. We ended up returning to Denver months later to film an episode at the Peabody-Whitehead Mansion, so I decided to bring Brendan along.

Why? Simple: Professional fighters have a different mentality than most people. Normal people don't make their living fighting in a cage with another trained warrior, and they don't have the courage to stand their ground against dark entities. Going into the kinds of places we do and accomplishing the mission of gathering paranormal evidence requires a trained body, mind, and spirit. Paranormal investigation at a high level takes a lot of dedication and preparation, and guys like Brendan have that edge. I also invited him along because I wanted to see how a modern-day warrior would react when he came face-to-face with one of these evil spirits.

What's interesting about the Peabody-Whitehead Mansion is the urban legend that some sort of rape and murder occurred in the basement during a renovation of the property. There is no factual data to support this story, and we said on air that it was unvalidated, but several people around the area spoke about it as if it were real. Not all legends are fiction, so we left our minds open to the idea that it could have happened.

Brendan came in full of smiles and great energy, so we took him down to the basement for a spirit box session. The spirit box is a controversial piece of equipment, but I believe in it. It scans AM and FM radio frequencies very rapidly (the same way a military radio frequency-hops) so we can tap into the radio waves portion of the electromagnetic spectrum. A major belief in the paranormal field is that ghosts are made up of electromagnetic energy. If that's true, then it stands to reason that they would try to communicate through the electromagnetic audio spectrum, and radio waves are in the electromagnetic spectrum. So if ghosts reside in the electromagnetic spectrum, then it makes sense to use radio waves to communicate with them, which is why the spirit box is so effective.

FUN FACT:

ELECTROMAGNETISM IS ONE OF THE FOUR FUNDAMENTAL FORCES IN THE UNIVERSE. THE OTHERS ARE GRAVITY, THE STRONG NUCLEAR FORCE, AND THE WEAK NUCLEAR FORCE.

We remove the antennas from our spirit boxes to eliminate the possibility of radio interference or noise contamination (critics seem to ignore that a lot). By doing so, we can let the device sweep with little to no chance of picking up any radio stations. The SB7 scans radio frequencies at such a high rate of speed—it can cover the entire radio spectrum in less than two seconds—that it's impossible to hear a coherent voice on one single frequency. There's a slim probability that a single syllable could come through, but it's virtually impossible for the spirit box to pick up multisyllabic words or phrases. And when the word or phrase that comes through is an intelligent answer to a direct question, you just can't chalk it up as radio interference. You can listen to nothing but white noise for hours with a spirit box without hearing a single blip of a DJ, music, or talk radio, even in the biggest metropolitan areas and next to powerful radio towers. This creates a contamination-free audio forum for nearby spirits to be heard.

Throughout the hundreds of investigations I've done, the rituals I've participated in, and the contacts I've made with the spirit world, the spirit box has been my favorite tool. I've put it through dozens of tests to prove to skeptics and myself that it legitimately captures spirit voices. I even hooked up two SB7 spirit boxes to two separate computer software programs so I could analyze the waveforms, and then swept a room at the Black Swan Inn. Both boxes were synchronized to sweep the same frequencies at the same time. Then I asked, "What was the lady's daughter's name?" The answer "Madison" came through one spirit box, which I could see on the waveform.

Why is that significant? Because if it was a random radio wave, then both boxes would have caught it, and it would have been visible on both waveforms. But since it was audible (and visible) on only one box, then the chances that it was a radio signal were exactly zero. Also, since it was the correct answer to the question I'd asked, that indicated intelligence, and I believe it was a great piece of paranormal evidence. I also used this device in the Perryville battlefield house, where I got the first and last name of a Civil War soldier, which was validated by the museum director as a casualty of the battle.

During a different investigation in Savannah, Georgia, we conducted a 90-minute spirit box session. Savannah is a large city with hundreds of radio stations, and during the entire hour and a half, we didn't get one single piece of contamination (or paranormal evidence, for that matter). If the spirit box was susceptible to out-side interference, as skeptics say, they would have picked up some-thing—anything—during that session, but it was completely quiet. The bottom line is this: It works and I believe in it.

Now back to Brendan Schaub. We brought him into the base-ment of the mansion, turned on a spirit box, and started asking questions, but nothing was coming through. It was quiet. Then I asked, "What happened to a girl down here?" and suddenly every-thing changed. "She was raped," a man's voice said, clear as any voice I've ever heard. I'd never seen a bad-ass heavyweight UFC fighter jump without his legs moving. It was like a cat sitting on a ledge that had a shoe thrown at it. After that, we got four more in-telligent answers related to this rape that we shared with the Denver police department. They even gave us permission to excavate the property to search for bodies, but the jury is still out on that one. I'm a paranormal investigator, not a paranormal excavator.

To put a cherry on this sundae, I asked the spirits what the name of the guy sitting next to me was, and a female spirit clearly said, "Brendan." It was awesome.

So the benefit of having guest investigators is that they bring a new energy to the room that spirits sometimes react to. Also, they're usually skeptics, so to see them react so positively to an event helps our credibility and shows our openness to bringing in outsiders. We've never had anything to hide and never will. We are not magicians or frauds or snake oil salesmen. We're credible investigators and are open to bringing outsiders in to prove that. And Brendan was a valuable addition to our team because he prepared himself properly and acted professional-ly. That's not always the case, though. Some guest investigators are...interesting.

In 2012, we investigated Frank Sinatra's private suite at the Riviera Hotel and Casino in Las Vegas, which is said to be haunted. Sinatra's parties were legendary, so we thought that if we threw a little party with musicians and women and even some of Frank's old friends, it would awaken the spirits there, maybe even Old Blue Eyes himself. So we invited someone Frank knew and partied with: Vince Neil, the lead singer of Motley Crüe.

We got a lot of bad press for Vince's appearance on the show because he was drinking during the investigation and showed up accompanied by several women. In his defense, it was meant to be this way. Sinatra was no teetotaler. He drank—a lot—so we wanted to create an atmosphere that he would have been comfortable in; we needed a party atmosphere with booze, women, and rock stars. We even brought in his old piano player and had him play some of Frank's favorite songs.

You have to remember that everyone thinks we should be a certain way as paranormal investigators. They're judgmental. Everyone has a preconceived notion of how we should act both in front of the camera and behind it. But spirits are intelligent. They're like us, but without bodies; they don't live in the material world anymore. So if you wanted to hang out with Sinatra or the people he hung out with back in the day, then would you go barging around his place with a bunch of gadgets, or would you show up with the things he liked and act the way he did?

Vince caught a lot of crap for drinking during the investigation and seeming drunk. (Aaron, Nick, and I did not drink anything, nor have we ever had alcohol during an investigation.) The alcohol factor was a challenge for me, because things were happening that were beyond my control. We always strive to be professional and responsible, and I knew this episode might not come across that way, but when I asked what hotel we were in, a woman's voice on the spirit box said, "Riviera." We also captured visual anomalies and EMF spikes. So did it work? I think it did, but nothing prepared me for when I broke off from the party with Vince and his girlfriend, Rain, and went to a different floor of the hotel.

At first we let Vince and Rain go off by themselves while we watched from the nerve center. While Vince was walking down the hallway, he was drawn to a particular room, and I remember thinking, "Wow, is Vince a sensitive?" He lost his daughter at a young age, so maybe that emotional event made him more spiritual or more in tune with the spirit world. Whatever it was, something drew him to this particular room. A few moments before, we'd caught a chilling voice on the spirit box, so there was paranormal energy in the air.

Vince Neil and I had a memorable experience with some ghosts at the Riviera.

By this point, Vince was more focused than he'd been at the party, so I joined him, and we went into the room that drew him in. As we entered, something went through both of us at the same time. It was like a spirit saw us coming in and decided to get out, but since we were in the doorway it had to go through us as well. Or maybe it was a spirit rushing over to hug us, for all I know. I can tell you that it was powerful. After the initial rush, I was overcome by sadness, and Vince collapsed on the ground.

A lot of people criticized Vince for that and said that he was drunk, but he absolutely was not. He was reacting to the spirit in the room, and I can verify that I felt it, too. Moments later, Vince complained that his left shoulder and arm were numb, which made me worry that he was having a heart attack. But my fears turned to amazement when I remembered that the coroner had told us several people had died of heart attacks on this floor of the hotel. So was Vince feeling the residual energy from one of those heart attacks? Possibly.

EITHER WAY, IT WAS A GREAT INVESTIGATION, AND HE WAS A VALUABLE GUEST WHOM I'M PROUD TO HAVE MET.

29

Sympathy, Said the Shark

A unique feature film that
I was proud to be a part of.

Devin Lawrence is like a brother to me. He's been an editor on *Ghost Adventures* for five years now, so I trust him. He edits the lockdown portions of our shows with me, so we basically see each other and work together all the time, because *GA* never stops. When we get home from a lockdown, Billy Tolley spends twelve to fourteen hours a day for four solid days watching all of our X-camera footage and listening to all of our audio and EVP sessions. In those four days, Billy finds unexplainable things that we build our edits around, and that's where Devin comes in. Devin comes to Vegas, and he and I get to work in the editing studio in my house. If we don't get any evidence, then we build the edit around how we conducted the investigation and all the innovative ways we tried to capture something. We've got it down to a science.

It didn't take me long to realize how talented Devin is as a filmmaker, and I saw long ago that he had more to offer than editing our lockdown footage. His edits are always 100 percent credible and authentic, and I wouldn't have it any other way. What you see on *GA* is real, and so is the evidence we capture. There is no fabrication of

213

any kind, because people like Devin make sure that we maintain strict standards.

One day I learned that Devin is also a screenwriter and has written many scripts. In September 2013, he told me that he had written a feature film script called *Sympathy, Said the Shark* and asked me to come aboard as an executive producer. I was very busy with *GA,* so I kept putting him off, much as I didn't want to. But since he's like family to me and I recognize his talent, I knew that this film would be something special. While TV is more my forte, I've always wanted to get into feature films, and I knew that if I got involved in Devin's project, it would be something we would both be proud of, and it would be a lot of fun.

I put down the majority investment, set up the production company, and did all the coordination to make his script a reality, but holy crap was it an insane process. Screenplays involve a lot more work than I anticipated—locations, sets, props, equipment, wardrobe, people, screenings, you name it. Devin had a director of photography picked out and had hired producers Casey Morris and Matt Mourgides, so the project was actually in pre-production when I came on board (thankfully). I went to LA and took on the task of casting with Devin, Casey, and Matt.

Casting was a lot of fun for me because I got to read from the script with the actors and help choose who would land each part. Believe it or not, we turned down Jim Belushi's son, Robert, and one of the stars of the TV show *Dexter.* These decisions led to some heated debates between Devin and me, but it all turned out for the best when we chose Dominic Bogart to play Church, Melinda Cohen to play Lara, and Lea Coco to play Justin. After going through the script, deciding on a visual look for the film, and talking with Devin about the innovative way he planned to film the whole thing, it was really fun to cast those people for those roles.

The type of film rig we used is the real breakthrough of this movie. It's a unique point-of-view camera rig designed by Devin and the film's director of photography, Mark LaFleur, and it truly is the most innovative thing ever. It's a motorcycle helmet fitted with a camera rig and a counterweight system that looks like the shrinking gun from *Honey, I Shrunk the Kids*. I've never seen anything like it, and Devin and Mark made it from scratch. The goal of this system is to see everything through the eyes of the lead actors, from a first-person point of view. I was there for the initial test runs, and I was amazed at the perspective it provides the viewer.

The actors wore the camera rig fitted with a remote-control follow focus, which meant that a cameraman could do the focusing back at video village where all the monitors were set up, and the directors and producers could watch what was going on and adjust the cameras remotely. This method of filming was a huge challenge for everyone involved with the movie. It was a risk, and whether or not we could pull it off was anyone's guess. It had never been done before, especially on the small budget we had to work with. My name was involved with this film (as was Devin's), not to mention the money I had riding on it, so this rig had to deliver. It was the biggest wow factor of the photography, and it had to be good.

> "[The movie] went from the initial concept to the script to casting within a year, and…we were always in that mode of, 'We are making this movie and we are bringing these pieces together.' It was like a runaway train where it just always kept moving. We really hit high gear probably in October when I went to Zak, and as soon as he got excited about it and came on board it just shot off. We went right into casting and we started filming at the end of December."
>
> —*Devin Lawrence,* Filmmaker Magazine *interview, July 2014*

The helmet weighed 15 pounds, and there were days when the actors would wear it for eight to ten hours a day. I can say from experience that being on camera is a demanding job, but actually *wearing* the camera is something else entirely. Some of the scenes were up to five minutes long, so they not only had to act out these long scenes, but wear a 15-pound helmet the entire time. Melinda even got injured once when a piece of the camera almost gouged her eye out, which was a scary moment.

As we were making the film, we were renting a house in northern LA and had a lot of issues with the homeowner. We took over his house for three weeks, filming all day and all night, and the whole time the hot-and-cold owner was picking fights with the

Our director of photography on the set, wearing the camera rig.

crew. At one point he almost got into a fistfight with a crew member who grabbed a pair of pliers to defend himself. I wasn't on set a lot since I was filming *GA* at the same time, but I got calls every day. I was constantly calling the homeowner and settling altercations, and over time the crew began referring to me as The Wolf, like the dude from *Pulp Fiction*. It was a madhouse.

I had a small part in the film, which was a lot of fun—and even a little dangerous. I played a guy who chases the Justin character (played by Lea Coco) after he steals my car. To film the car chase, I rode in a pickup truck while Lea sped away from me in my own Dodge Challenger (the same one from the Pioneer Saloon episode of *Ghost Adventures*). Was I nervous about using my own car? You bet. Especially when things went very wrong.

In this scene, I was in the passenger seat of the truck with two thugs. We filmed it on a remote road north of LA (in Santa Clarita, the same city where *The Fast and the Furious* actor Paul Walker died and we filmed the Heritage Junction episode of *GA*). We started filming early in the morning, and Devin was sick as a dog. He had a high fever and looked like death, but he was still there. He's a true professional. The scene involved me hanging out the window and yelling at this guy that I was going to kick his ass. Six takes went fine, but the seventh one didn't.

Since we weren't big-time enough to stop traffic during filming, there were cars on the road that day. Matt Mourgides was driving the truck, and we were following the Challenger and swerving on a one-way road. Matt cut the wheel hard left, and my door suddenly flew open at 45 miles an hour. I reached out and grabbed the window frame just in time to keep myself from splattering all over the road. I remember looking down and seeing the road whizzing by and thinking, "This can't be my time." Obviously it wasn't, but when it was over and we stopped, I was shaken up. It was a really close call, and I had to take some time to calm down afterward.

I should take this opportunity to make an apology. Later I got to appear in another scene where my character pulls the Justin character out of the Challenger, and in every take I hurt our star, Lea Coco, because his stomach would scrape against the door.

SORRY, BRO.

On the set of *Sympathy, Said the Shark.*
You can see the pickup truck I nearly fell out of.

30

BEHIND THE CAMERA

So you want to be
a documentary filmmaker?

I've made two feature-length documentary films. The original *Ghost Adventures,* released in 2004, won the Grand Jury Prize for Best Documentary at the New York International Independent Film and Video Festival and was nominated for Best Feature Film at the Erie Horror Film Festival. I was young and inexperienced in film-making when I made it; like any artist, I've gotten better with time and experience. Making that documentary (and all 100-something episodes of the show that we've done since) sculpted my mind and trained me to become a better filmmaker. My next feature documentary, *The Demon House,* which will be released in 2015, is amazing.

Being a documentary filmmaker is kind of like being an entertainer, like a singer or an actor. A lot of people want to be world-famous entertainers, but only a few have that magic something that helps them achieve it. They have a special presence in front of the camera, or an indescribable sound on the microphone. They can give themselves completely to the performance and take the story or song to a whole new level.

Documentary filmmaking is kind of like that. A good filmmaker can open up a story that people think they know the end to and add something meaningful to it. It's like being an investigative reporter; you have to be able to search through your topic, find new twists and turns, and develop the story into a more dynamic experience. You have to dissect your topic so much that you end up adding more to the story than it had originally.

For example, when I found the woman who lived in the Demon House in the 1980s, she told me that she would have violent nightmares and that someone would die soon afterward, which added a huge plot twist. Her experiences built on and expanded the story and opened a door for a good documentary filmmaker to explore. Then I brought her to the house where she was attacked and her daughter was later possessed, which added a whole new story line to the original foundation and made the film so much more fascinating.

There are two types of documentaries: original stories and familiar stories told in a new and insightful way. *The Demon House* is original. No one has done it. "Who killed JFK?" has been done, but that doesn't mean a good filmmaker couldn't find a new angle or piece of evidence that would shed new light on the story.

To be a successful filmmaker, you have to be good at many different things. You have to be a great interviewer, producer, and director, and if you're lacking in any one of those areas, the whole project will crumble. The ability to glue all the pieces together and make a flowing story that grabs the audience's attention and doesn't let go is absolutely critical. You have to be able to take what you've found in your investigations and develop it into something more— take an interview or a piece of research and dig deeper so that when all these puzzle pieces are brought together, they make your story unforgettable. That's where you succeed or fail: You either have that ability or you don't, and if you don't, no one will watch the film, and all your work will be for nothing.

A make-it-or-break-it aspect of documentary filmmaking is finding your own creative vision for the picture and figuring out how you're going to set the mood for presenting it. For me, setting a tone with a certain look brings the story to life. *The Demon House* is uncomfortable and uninviting on purpose. Because the topic is demons, which are cold, dirty, dark, and evil, I wanted the atmospheric shots to reflect that cold nature. To give the film an icy look, I used a lot of blues and grays and wintry environmental details like snow and icicles. I wanted industrial coal factories, abandoned buildings, and dead crops to enhance the sense of decay. The geographic shots are isolated, abandoned, and cold, with few people in them, so the film has a post-apocalyptic feel to it. When you're

cold and alone, you're quiet and huddled up and hiding from the air itself. I think that mood is perfect for this film.

When I shoot the landscape, I use visual metaphors to enhance my storytelling. I find objects that speak to the mood or emotions I'm trying to evoke in the audience. A dead possum on the side of the road or a rundown playground overrun with weeds or covered in ice—those visual metaphors mean something. The possum means death. The playground says poverty. These images work perfectly in *The Demon House*.

I've always been a visual person. I never learned from reading; I learn by seeing or doing things. When I interview people, I can see their words and envision what they're saying. That makes it easier to put their words into images or to create reenactments of key events. When we put together an episode of *Ghost Adventures*, we always include interviews and stories because I think the audience learns better that way. Instead of talking to someone, you show them pictures, and they remember them. That's the way my mind works, and I try to carry it over into my TV shows and films.

The one thing I truly love about documentary filmmaking is that there is no script. Movies are great, but I could never be a feature film director. A feature film is a play that follows a script, with set roles and no freedom. Maybe that says something about me. Maybe I don't like boundaries, and I thrive in an environment where I can make things up as I go. I like guerrilla reporting, being out in the field and not knowing what's going to happen that day. I like the rush of doing an interview and seeing it open a new door. I like being in a small car with a familiar crew driving toward the unknown, with our cameras ready to roll.

As a documentary filmmaker, you have to be the force that makes things happen. You have to dare yourself to push the limits of the story to create something incredible. You have to see how far you can push your investigation—a good documentary filmmaker knows no boundaries. You have to get out there and interview people. You have to know how to look for leads and follow up on those leads that take you from one interview to another to another to another. Each of those interviews gets you deeper and deeper into the story, to the point where you're embedded in it and you may even be in danger, for all you know. Or you discover new information that no other media outlet has been able to uncover. Like a detective, you've got to have a mind, ear, eye, and voice for it.

A documentary filmmaker also needs to have a great memory. With a regular movie that follows a script, you know exactly what you have to shoot and how you're going to piece it all together. A documentary could take one, two, or five years to film and involve hundred or even thousands of hours of footage. That makes it hard to figure out where to start when it's time to put it together. A lot of documentary films fail because the filmmaker doesn't have the memory (or filing system) to know where certain bits and pieces of footage are. You have to log everything you've shot and remember it all. You have to be organized, because when it comes time for editing, you have to go back through all those of hours of footage and put it together into a smooth, compelling story. This is where some people quit. A lot of documentary filmmakers get lost in the editing and can't remember what they shot or where to start or how to connect all the pieces.

You also have to be a writer. A documentary filmmaker writes the narrations that lead the audience from one puzzle piece to the next (called transitions). During the filming of *Netherworld,* I did a lot of moody writing that supported how I wanted the overall visual presentation to come off. *Netherworld* was artistic, with abstract visuals and hints of electronic music, so the moody writing was perfect for it. (Flip back to chapter 13 for more on that adventure.)

A great documentary filmmaker has to put together a great crew and be a great leader for that crew. You have to know what you want from them, be strict and organized, and know how to bring out their best. And speaking of people, you can't let anything or anyone affect your creativity or color your vision for the film. A strong filmmaker doesn't compromise his standards or let other people run the show. A weak person may not be able to handle a certain shoot or a particular person, so he ends up being more lenient on the production itself. This is not and never will be me or the people I work with. I make sure to bring in only the most professional and dedicated people who understand my vision for a project, which has been a big part of my success.

You have to make sure that everything you shoot—every interview, every piece of B-roll footage—follows your direction and is in line with your creative vision. You can't let anyone mess with that. A documentary is a hunt to find the end of your story. It's a mission, and you can never let go of it or give up on it. If you do, you can give away your title as a documentary filmmaker. You've lost your dignity and let yourself down.

No matter what the circumstances, a great filmmaker finds a way to get it done. If you run into financial problems or some other major hurdle, you can't give up. *Ghost Adventures* (the film) was shot on a shoestring budget, but I never let that interfere with the storytelling. You have to be *Braveheart* about it and fight for your freedom. Ironically, though, I don't recommend documentary filmmaking as a career. It's not easy, and in some cases you put your life on the line to carry out your vision.

IT'S A TOUGH BUSINESS THAT EATS ITS YOUNG.

31

Ex-Girlfriends' Ghosts

Women are hard enough to handle without their ghosts, too.

Some guys say, "All my exes live in Texas." For me, all my exes get haunted and freaked out by evil spirits. It's the nature of dating me. Over a period of two years, every girl I dated was affected by the spirit attachments I had during that time. I couldn't help it. Every time I came back from an investigation, I seemed to bring back baggage that would attack whoever I was dating. It was awful. Over those two years, I'd say twelve women were affected in some way, and half of them experienced severe attacks. Dealing with women is hard enough. Demons make it nearly impossible.

A spiritual healer from Hungary told me that I had a possessive female spirit following me around and a demonic attachment. I don't doubt it. In fact, two separate healers came up with this same diagnosis, and neither one knew the other, so I believe it. It made sense to me, so for a while I had all the women I dated sign waivers so I wouldn't be responsible for anything that happened to them.

I'm joking.

When the attacks died down, I thought it was over. In the past year I haven't had any paranormal activity at my house, which is a

225

big relief since before then, every woman was getting attacked in some way when she came over. But recently, an ex-girlfriend called me out of the blue to tell me that she was having severe experiences with a spirit at home. Two weeks later, another woman said the same thing. No, there's no way they could have collaborated on this. They don't know about each other, have never met, and live in different states.

Coincidence? C'mon. Look who we're talking about here.

The first girlfriend (we'll call her Ms. Blue) had a serious problem, and I had to go to her apartment because things were getting so bad. I hadn't seen her in a long time, so yeah, it was awkward, but I wanted to help. So I went over one night to see what was going on. Apparently a spirit was attacking her and her roommate. It also damaged the apartment itself, tearing down the blinds, raising the washing machine lid, turning lights on and off, and opening and closing doors, and taunted Ms. Blue while she was sleeping. As soon as I walked into the apartment, I could feel that something wasn't right. The air was heavy, and we definitely weren't alone.

I've done this job for many years now, and I've conducted hundreds of interviews with people who have been traumatized by spirits. Ms. Blue and her roommate were legitimately freaked out and concerned for their well-being (it wasn't a booty call, for those of you who may be wondering). So I walked in, sat down on the couch, started talking to them, and immediately felt uneasy.

It was worse upstairs in the bedrooms. I couldn't even stay in Ms. Blue's room because something unfriendly was there, pushing me out like it knew I could sense it and fight it. It wasn't as strong in her roommate's room, but it was still there, so we went downstairs to talk. That's when things got worse.

I'm a sensitive and an empath and can channel the emotions of the spirits around me, and this one was angry. Really angry. Within seconds I was aggravated and wanted to do the women harm, and I knew that the negative energy wasn't coming from me. Something was trying to make me feel its rage. Luckily I recognized what was going on and got out before I could cause any trouble. Outside the apartment, I told them that something was in there and it wasn't good, and they needed to leave before it affected them permanently. I had gone over there just to reassure them that everything was okay, but I was unprepared for what I found.

The thing is, after I dated Ms. Blue, she had a bad relationship with a man who got her into trouble. He was a bad influence and almost destroyed her life—the kind of guy you wouldn't want around your daughter, like Mark Wahlberg's character in the movie *Fear*. About six months before the night I went to her apartment to see what was going on, he was shot and killed, so my first thought was that this spirit was him coming back to dominate her from the other side. He seemed like a usual suspect, and that's who you always start with.

But then two weeks later, another ex-girlfriend (we'll call her Ms. Green) texted me with almost the *exact* same story. It matched Ms. Blue's nearly word for word—damaged blinds, doors opening and closing, lights turning on and off, the works. Did I think it was a conspiracy? Sure. But trust me, there's no way these women could have cooked up this story between them, especially since I felt the spirit at Ms. Blue's apartment and knew she wasn't faking it. They don't even know each other. So how was it that they were having the same issues?

And then it hit me. Could the same spirit have moved from Ms. Blue's apartment to Ms. Green's? Did the attachment travel from one place to the other? Remember what I said about the possessive female spirit that attacked women in my house? Hell hath no fury like a jealous woman, right? Could it be that this malevolent spirit remembered them from when they would come to my house and was trying to terrorize them both? Could it be that it was trying to feed off their fear and knew that it could manipulate me by getting me involved? It's like a funky triangle of jealousy. It's the worst kind of love triangle you can imagine—one with a demon chick involved…literally. She's baaaaaaaaaack.

Fortunately, the attacks have subsided (at the time this book is being published, at least). Sometimes hauntings last a long time, and sometimes they last only a short while and then go away: The entity gets what it wants and then leaves the victim(s) alone. I didn't really do anything to stop them, but the attacks ended, which is fine by me. But let this be a warning to any woman who wants to date me. I'm not a stalker, but some sort of bitchy spirit watching over me is.

GEORGE STRAIT'S EXES MAY LIVE IN TEXAS, BUT MINE GET POSSESSED.

32

CRAZY FANS

Some of you scare me.

I have a dungeon that has become my refuge, and many days I just want to stay there. We all need a safe harbor where we can get away from everything and feel secure. Since I am a fan of Dracula and the dark bits of life, it was only fitting for me to remodel my basement into a dungeon when I had some extra money. It's me, and it's the one place I can retreat to when I've had enough of everything—especially people who have no boundaries.

I was filming an episode of *Paranormal Challenge* at the Trans-Allegheny Lunatic Asylum in West Virginia when Dave Schrader, Chris Fleming, and I decided to get something to eat at McDonald's. (Don't judge me.) It was evening, and we were done filming for the day. Since Weston, West Virginia, is a small town, we figured we would sit inside and eat. What could happen, right?

As we strode across the parking lot, I noticed one of those old child molester vans in the back of the lot. It looked like the A-Team van from the early 1980s, except this one had no windows, so I was a little on edge with each step—and with good reason, it turned out. When we were about halfway to the door of the McDonald's, the sliding door of the van opened, and two women came running toward us.

"Zak, you need to say hello to my daughter," the older woman said.

"Hello," I said.

"Do you not recognize her?"

I was starting to feel uneasy. Seeing the way they carried themselves, I could tell that something about them was off, and not in a good way. "No, I don't recognize her," I replied. The girl, who was probably fifteen or sixteen, suddenly covered her face with her hands and burst into tears.

Oh boy. Here we go.

"Well, Zak, you've been having sex with my daughter through astral projection, and now she's pregnant!"

And there it was.

Dave Schrader has been around a lot of strange people and could see right away that this wasn't a good situation. He took charge and told the woman to leave or we would call the police, then ushered Chris and me inside. A few moments and a couple of comments later, they complied and went back to their van, while we went into Mickey D's to laugh it off over some Big Mac goodness. All good, right?

Nope.

Twenty minutes later, the van returned, and I envisioned the sliding door opening and a machine gun opening fire on us. Seriously, the mother was clearly ten cents short of a two-dollar bill, and she didn't seem to care how far the situation might escalate. As she marched toward the door of the McDonald's, I got angrier with every step she took. I don't want to be harassed while I'm trying to enjoy a meal with my friends, and I won't shy away from a confrontation to stand up for my privacy. We met her in the entryway, and this woman proceeded to repeat that her daughter was crying because she'd been astral projecting herself and having a sexual relationship with me in the astral plane for a long time, and now she was expecting our love child. Someone was cuckoo for Cocoa Puffs.

FUN FACT:

THE ASTRAL PLANE IS A THEORETICAL PLANE OF EXISTENCE THAT MANY RELIGIONS BELIEVE SOULS CROSS OVER BEFORE BEING BORN AND AFTER DEATH. SOME BELIEVE THAT THE ASTRAL PLANE CAN BE VISITED CONSCIOUSLY THROUGH ASTRAL PROJECTION, MEDITATION AND MANTRA, NEAR-DEATH EXPERIENCE, LUCID DREAMING, OR OTHER MEANS. SOME CLAIM THAT THEY CAN USE THE "ASTRAL VEHICLE" TO SEPARATE THEIR CONSCIOUSNESS FROM THE PHYSICAL BODY AND TRAVEL THROUGH THE ASTRAL PLANE, BUT HAVING SEX ACROSS IT? THAT WOULD BE AN INCREDIBLE FEAT OF METAPHYSICS.

Dave and I calmly pointed out how crazy this story sounded and how she should listen to what she was implying. Only the Holy Spirit can impregnate women without physical contact. I am not the Holy Spirit, and I was pretty sure that neither was her daughter. We again implored her to leave before the police came, and thankfully she did without resorting to violence, but I was on edge the whole time. Some people are good at hiding their intentions and will swing into unpredictability at a moment's notice. I kept expecting her to do something rash, but thankfully she never did. I never saw those two again, but I'll never look at a Big Mac the same way.

Unfortunately, the paranormal world attracts a lot of people like this. Though I suspect that every field of entertainment has its fair share of eccentrics, there seems to be a large concentration of bizzaro characters in the paranormal world. I guess I shouldn't be surprised. I don't know if it's the subject of death or the spiritual side of life that attracts oddballs, but we seem to flock to it...myself included. I'm not normal and I never have been, but that doesn't mean it's okay to get obsessed with me, like this next person did.

Dave Schrader used to host events through his Darkness Radio platform where he would invite 300 to 500 fans to spend three days at a haunted location with us and some of our friends in the paranormal profession, like Jeff Belanger and Mark and Debby Constantino. Anyone could come and greet us at a social get-together, listen to lectures on the paranormal, participate in a ghost hunt, and help raise money for charity. While it was a great time for everyone and 99 percent of the fans were great, there was always that 1 percent who were better suited to *America's Most Wanted* than *Ghost Adventures*.

A couple years ago we were doing one of these events at the Stanley Hotel in Colorado. The Stanley is a beautiful estate nestled in the mountains about two hours outside of Denver. It's famous for being the hotel where Stephen King had a paranormal experience that inspired him to write *The Shining*. Though it's definitely haunted, it's not a very violent place, so it's a perfect environment for bringing in fans with little or no paranormal experience. On the first night we did an auction to raise money for local charities. (That part isn't relevant to the story. I'm just proud to say it.) I was passing through the hotel lobby after the auction when a woman stopped me and asked if she could show me a picture she had painted of me. I said sure, and I thought it was a really cool gesture—until she pulled out a painting of an empty room.

"Is this someplace I've investigated?" I asked.

"No. This is the room you're going to die in," she answered.

"Excuse me?"

"Yeah. This is the room you're going to die in, of respiratory failure."

It's amazing how fast the human mind can switch from happiness to hellfire rage. I went off. I couldn't help it. Something about this incident really incensed me, and I lost my mind. I yelled at her to get out of the building before Chris Fleming, who has a knack for getting between me and crazy fans, stepped in to calm me down. Some people think that I won't stand up for myself—that because I'm a public figure, they can say what they want and I'll just laugh it off because I don't want to be seen losing my cool on TMZ, but they're wrong. I'll defend myself if I feel threatened, and I won't care about the damage it causes until later. Part of me regrets blowing up at her, but another part of me doesn't.

When this happened, I honestly wasn't sure whether this woman was possessed by a demon that was trying to torture me. Chris got the same feeling, and I've learned to trust his instincts. It may explain why I got so mad so fast. I don't know what Chris did to get rid of the woman, but I saw him a little while later, and he just said that he had resolved the situation, like some bad-ass sniper.

Okay, one more crazy fan story. I have a hundred of them. I'm not trying to ridicule anyone, but you just can't make this stuff up, and there's a point to it all eventually.

The scene was Scarefest 2013 in St. Louis. Scarefest draws a lot of people and is a great time, but because I'm an empath and a sensitive, it can also be a daunting adventure in sensory overload for me. When hundreds of people are standing in line to meet me, I can feel their emotions and energy, and it's overwhelming. It's like being in the middle of a loud, crowded rave with lights flashing and bass thumping. Your senses are assaulted from all sides, and there's no way out. Just like a paranormal investigation, an event like Scarefest where I interact with hundreds of people is totally draining, and when it's over I want to crawl into bed for a week or get lost in Red Rock Canyon.

I've always enjoyed Scarefest, though. It's run well, and they go out of their way to make me feel comfortable and secure. In 2009 I had just filed a restraining order against the craziest fan of all time, who had threatened to show up at Scarefest and kill me. So the organizers made sure that I had two jolly green giants escorting me everywhere I went. It was overkill, but you never know when someone is going to follow through on a threat, and then everyone is left to say, "We should have seen it coming." So I appreciate what they did for me.

At the 2013 show, I arrived early and went to check out my booth. I noticed that there was no security, and the VIP ticket holders were allowed to walk freely around the main floor before the show started. I was cool with that. But while I was setting up the booth, a strange woman approached and showed me a collection of photos of me in various places—photos I'd never seen before. She had pictures of me doing everyday things like getting juice at a health food store and hanging out with a friend. It was like a private investigator's file or something.

"You better watch yourself," she said.

"Excuse me?"

"I know someone who's photographing your house in Vegas and your cars when the garage is open and every facet of your life."

Like I was during the encounter with the woman who said that I was going to die of respiratory failure in the room she'd painted, I was instantly angry. This woman may have been mentally off, but I don't tolerate this sort of stuff. I genuinely like to meet fans and hang out with the people who have made myself and the show popular, but not if it means putting up with threats or being bullied.

I'm not taking time out of my life to interact with people who just want to harass me.

As you may have noticed, I have a short fuse. I don't ever want to blow up and do something stupid that's going to get me in trouble. I know this about myself, so I brought a friend with me to Scarefest who's about 6'8" and 280 pounds. He told the woman to leave, and she did, but she continued to cause problems throughout the event. All weekend she spread rumors that people were watching me and I was doomed. It was disturbing, and I wasn't happy about her having unrestricted access to me, so that was the last time I attended Scarefest. It's unfortunate that one fan can ruin it for everyone else, but that's the way it goes sometimes.

I am very confident in the way I stay protected.

Some people just don't have any boundaries or filters and go out of their way to try to hurt you for whatever sick reason they're harboring. I don't want to get shot by a disgruntled stalker or, even worse, see a fan get caught in the crossfire when a stalker comes after me, so I stay in my house 90 percent more than I used to. But you know what? I asked for this life, so I have to deal with all the trappings that come with it.

In the end, anyone who has achieved a modicum of fame has to realize that you will never have a normal life again. You just have to suck it up and deal with it. I worked hard to get into the limelight, and now I have to deal with the unpleasantness that it brings into my life. The alternative is never to leave the house, which is almost where I am at this point. I used to get excited about meeting people and sharing stories and theories about the paranormal, but I've been crossed by so many people with an axe to grind that it's made me jaded and gun-shy. I hate that, but it's just the way things are now. We all make sacrifices to get what we want, and for me to make *Ghost Adventures* successful means that I don't have any privacy. Ever.

UNLESS I'M IN MY DUNGEON.

33

SOUTHWEST HELL

Wrong place at the wrong time.

I hate flying for many reasons, but mostly because it does one very weird thing to me. Every time I fly I have to pee...a lot. Someone can just say the word *water* and I'm sprinting to the lavatory in mid-flight. I'm sure there's some sort of medical name for it, like depressurized bladder syndrome, but the last thing I want to do is see a doctor about it. That's a waste of healthcare dollars. I just suck it up and sit in the aisle seat so I can get there faster.

When I fly (which I do a lot), I usually have to pee six to eight times during a two-hour flight. And when I do get up and go to the lavatory, I can't pee, even though I have to. So I stand there listening to the flight attendants do their thing just outside the lavatory, with nothing happening for me down below. Then I start imagining that there is no wall and I'm standing there with 200 people staring at me. And then I get scared that one of the doors will break open and I'll get sucked out of the lavatory with my wiener hanging out, or maybe the suction of the toilet will pull me out of the plane. It's like a whole new bag of crazy stage fright or social anxiety disorder. I hate it.

When I get back to my seat, eight times out of ten I hit my head on the overhead compartment, and it's like Keystone Cops theater with the whole plane full of passengers watching me. It's impossible to play it off when 200 bored people see you ram your forehead into a piece of plastic with a loud THUMP and laugh at your pain. So the bottom line is, I hate flying, especially when something goes wronger than wrong.

I was coming home to Vegas on Southwest Airlines after filming an episode. I was in the front row of the plane in the aisle seat so I could get to the lavatory quickly each and every time I took a drink of anything. It was just another flight, except for one thing...the flight attendant was gorgeous. I mean Danica Patrick hot. And on top of that, she was super nice to everyone. Like genuinely nice, and not in an "I'm being nice to you because I have to" kind of way. I don't make snap judgments, and I sure wasn't on a love quest, but I definitely had a little high-altitude crush going on.

We were getting ready to land, and once again I had to go to the bathroom. We were descending rapidly, so I knew that if I didn't go right away, I'd be holding it for a long, painful spell. You know the deal: After landing, the plane has to taxi, and then we all wait until they bring out the jetway and open the doors, and by the time I get to a bathroom inside the airport, I'm probably standing in a pool of my own urine. No way that was going to happen, especially not in front of this perfect ten. I was going to go even if I had to barrel through a platoon of air marshals to get there. You're not supposed to get up after the "Stay in your seats under penalty of death" light goes on, but I wasn't having it. But if I had known then what I know now, I would have stayed put.

I got up, went to the lavatory, locked the door, and lifted up the toilet seat, and there he was: Mister Stankie. A big, nasty log of shit was clinging to the side of the toilet. I got a noseful of it and...oh dear God. I was nearly sick to my stomach and had absolutely no desire to pee anymore. I didn't dare touch the flush button, because I assumed that whoever had the gall to lay down this redwood log of doom and not make sure that it got flushed probably didn't wash his hands, either. I had one driving mission at that point: to get out fast. I turned and bolted with the toilet seat still up and the log still maintaining its death clutch to the side of the bowl. I should have tried to get rid of it so the next person wouldn't have to see it, but I was too grossed out. It was self-preservation.

But as I came out of the lavatory, I looked down the aisle and saw the super-hot flight attendant walking toward me from the rear of the airplane. At first I didn't care, but as I clicked my seat belt it hit me. She was heading toward the lavatory!

A million things flashed through my mind, none of them good. This was a really bad situation. She was going to come up there and check out the lavatory and think I laid down that log. She didn't see how long I was in there. She didn't know that I'd walked in and walked right back out again. She was going to think that I went in there and took a giant shit and didn't flush. Panic set in. I grabbed the media control handle on my armrest and thought of all those silly video game combinations to unlock a secret move. Maybe left-left-up-down-spin-spin-kick would eject me from the social hell I was in, which only got deeper with each step she took.

The seconds ticked away like an eternity as she slowly made her way to the front of the plane. I was in the front row and had no seat to hide behind as she reached the front and started doing flight attendant things. I started sweating. I was moments away from a full-fledged panic attack. She put the trash in a bag and turned all the red switches on the control panels and did all the stuff they do to prep for landing. Maybe I'd get lucky. Maybe she wouldn't...

But then she did. She opened the door to the lavatory, and my worst fears came true. She looked in the toilet and saw what I saw: Mister Stankie staring back at her, meaner and smellier than ever. She turned to me with the most disgusted look on her face, and I knew that any chance I had to meet her was flushed (pun intended). To add insult to injury, she balanced on one leg, lifted the other to the flush button like a Cirque du Soleil performer, and hit it with her toes while her gorgeous face frowned the frown of eternal damnation. At that point, I didn't care if the plane crashed like a lawn dart.

I have never taken, and will never take, a dump on an airplane. I can barely pee, and in the many hundreds of flights I've taken in my life, I've never once felt the urge to go number two, no matter how long the flight was. I'm fine with people who do it, but for Chrissakes, flush. Not flushing is like blowing your nose in your hand and then shaking my hand—it's just not right.

I took the blame for that log, and it wasn't even mine. I wanted to stand up and tell the flight attendant that it was the guy two rows back whom I'd seen go in there a minute before I did. As if this nightmare couldn't drag on any longer, it did. She kept flushing, but the demon poo refused to go down, like it was attached to the bowl with some sort of crazy monkey glue compound. With every flush, I descended to another level of hell...and not the kind I'm used to.

To this day it still bugs me a little, because she probably tells her friends about that disgusting guy from *Ghost Adventures* who didn't flush, and they all laugh about it while watching my show. We all have embarrassments like this that we want to forget. It was a horrible moment of being in the wrong place at the wrong time that will stick with me forever.

I HATE FLYING.

34

THE DEVIL

Just leave him alone.

The paranormal field has more questions than answers, and working in it day after day can be maddening. So many times I feel like I'm on the edge of a discovery but end up right back where I started. Religion is especially tricky. My years of poking and prodding the very basis of our existence have convinced me that God and Jesus do exist, but when you believe that, you have to acknowledge that the other side must exist, too. It's not easy to admit that the devil is real. I've been there, and I can tell you that he's as bad as people say he is.

So many people pray every day. Prayer is a ritual that involves certain movements and postures: bowing the head, making the sign of the cross, holding hands together in humility. It's one ritual of many in the church. There are rituals for taking the holy sacrament, rituals for confessing sins, rituals for joining together in holy matrimony, and many others, depending on your denomination. Houses of worship everywhere welcome millions upon millions of people who feel that they have a relationship with God and ask for forgiveness of their sins.

So where does sin come from? Is it human nature, or does the devil try to influence the world by making people sin? And why do some people commit more extreme sins than others? Abuse, corruption, violence, murder—these are all ways I believe the devil feeds. The spiritual battle between God and the devil is always at work, every day, every minute, every second. When a possession occurs, we see this struggle firsthand. We see supernatural things happen: the possessed person levitating and speaking in tongues, holy water scarring the skin, evil being cast out by good. It's powerful.

So what happens to those who seek God? If they worship God wholeheartedly and lead holier lives than others, does God give them the gift of tranquility and erase all violence from them? Does God make them pure, and do they live more peaceful lives? I bet many of them do. Do I have a deep connection with God and Christ? I would say that I do, but at times I question it. I ask the same question that atheists and agnostics always ask: why God or Jesus would allow so much pain to happen in life, especially to innocent children. My faith isn't shaken, but I continually ask why these awful things are allowed to go on. If God created life, then why doesn't He maintain it? Why doesn't He show us His Godly power and correct the things that are happening in the life He gave us? It's not anti-religious or wrong to question God. I pray sometimes. I wonder whether anyone hears it, but I believe that there's a cleansing power in prayer. It reminds your body that there's something beyond its confines. You can train yourself through prayer. Just like everyone wants me to show them a ghost or spirit, people want to hear and feel God to believe in Him, so they pray and hope that those prayers are answered.

Funny thing: I question God and Jesus, but I don't question exorcists. I've seen so many exorcisms. They're powerful. They invoke the name of God to eradicate a demon from a living body. I've had a demon inside me and felt the stinging and burning when holy water was sprinkled on my forehead. In that moment, I felt God, and lately I've been thinking more and more about how evil spirits and entities can try to make you sick and even kill you (though to be fair, good spirits can also do you harm if they try to use your energy or channel through you).

And what about the people who try to pursue the devil—not necessarily to worship the devil, but to explore it? Demonologists are usually very religious individuals who only seek to understand the devil. Why wouldn't they? It's only natural to want to find the answers to our questions about religion and explore what lies beyond God and Jesus. To do that, we have to go where the action is, and where's that? On a battlefield. And where is the battlefield between God and the devil? Exorcisms.

Exorcisms are ground zero for the struggle between good and evil. Both sides fight fiercely to control an innocent human being—a pure soul who has no desire to be part of the battle. It's usually a soul with a lot of potential that the devil wants to control and the angels want to leave alone to live a peaceful and productive life. The body becomes the battlefield, but there are other battlefields, too—real ones made of earth and stone that humans, whether they mean to or not, sometimes mess with, opening up a portal that should have been left undisturbed.

When we went to Ireland to film for *Ghost Adventures,* we decided to research and try to interpret some of the ancient legends, and to attempt to find the devil himself. Ireland is such an intriguing place. So many mysterious things have happened on these ancient lands, and still do. There were the Druids, an ancient Celtic people whose religious leaders seemed to understand the struggle between good and evil and got themselves mixed up in it. To this day, historians don't understand much about the Druids and the rituals they performed, but some accounts say that those rituals involved human sacrifice. When Christianity came to the Emerald Isle and everyone turned their attention to Jesus, it's said that the mythological creatures, gods, and goddesses buried themselves in the ground, where they still lie dormant, waiting for the right time to reappear.

To travel to lands that are home to ancient burial grounds and stone passageways and grave cairns is amazing. These kinds of places are found all over the island, and there's so much that's unknown about these ancient peoples and their religious practices. It's like layer upon layer of questions with no answers. Two of these sites—the Hellfire Club atop Montpelier Hill in County Dublin and Loftus Hall to the south—are said to have been visited by the devil himself. These stories have been passed down for centuries, so they seemed like the right places for us to begin our investigations. But then the shit hit the fan.

We tried to summon Satan. We tried to call him out. I hate to admit it, but we thought we could pull it off, and I witnessed one of the most disturbing things I've ever seen since I started doing this job, and it may have permanently affected one of my best friends.

The Ghost Adventures Crew doesn't live by a code book for paranormal investigating. Some other paranormal groups think that you have to live by a set of rules, and everybody has to investigate this way or that way. People preach that there's one right way to investigate. That's like some backwater group telling a priest how to pray. It just doesn't make sense, and they look stupid when they try to force their investigation methods on others.

Now, I won't be a hypocrite and suggest that we don't have our own processes and standards that we share with our GAC-affiliated crews. We've been doing this a long time, and we've developed many effective techniques for conducting paranormal research. But there are groups who are so set in their ways that they aren't flexible enough to adapt to different situations and end up missing out on great opportunities. Every haunted location is different. What works in one place may not work in another. Spirits are people without physical bodies, and every person, living or dead, is an individual.

Bruce Lee was the true father of mixed martial arts, and he taught his students this philosophy: Don't let yourself be so rigid and inflexible that you can't adapt to your opponent. When it comes time to fight, be like water and flow. Let the environment dictate how you move, not the other way around. The same can be said for paranormal investigation. Every place and every ghost is unique, and you have to be able to adapt. In the end, the results are more important that the process. Evidence and progress are what count the most.

Now, there are groups out there that take this job to extreme levels, vandalizing property and mutilating themselves and other ridiculous bullshit, and I agree that they're not doing it right. But the GAC tries hard to let investigators be investigators and move the field forward. We like to expand ourselves by participating in rituals and having emotional experiences, just as people go to church and pray to better themselves. Just as they seek to calibrate themselves to have an experience with God, we calibrate ourselves to connect to the spirits.

But we may have taken it too far in Ireland.

We were on top of Montpelier Hill at the Hellfire Club. At the top of this hill there's a beautiful old hunting lodge that was built around 1725 by a wealthy man who used stones from a nearby passage grave. The story goes that he had no idea what he'd done. Not only were the stones taken from a prehistoric burial ground, but the woods surrounding the lodge were said to be filled with ancient demons and creatures that had buried themselves there when

Christianity came. It's said that the devil himself visited the lodge and blew off the roof just after it was completed. Years later, the secretive satanic Hellfire Club held its rituals there to call upon the devil. It's said that Satan appeared in the lodge during a card game among the members in cloven feet and fireballs. It sounds kind of crazy, but it's right up my alley.

So we investigated this lodge and went through the ritual to summon Satan when something unexpected and terrifying happened: We got an answer. First we captured rocks and glass moving and the sound of a claw scratching across something, probably the ground. Then something happened to Aaron. He claimed he felt a claw-hand firmly grab his ear and pull it backward with force, along with a powerful jolt of dark energy, and he believes to this day that Satan touched his ear. Later, I asked the spirits who touched Aaron, and a woman's voice said, "Satan." It was the only voice we got that night, and we knew immediately that we'd pushed it too far.

I saw my friend in a state of absolute panic, which I'd never seen before. He started crying, and for once in my life I had no idea what to do. I was truly disturbed to see my friend in such agony because I knew that something very powerful was present in the Hellfire Club and lashed out at him. I was very concerned for Aaron because earlier in the day he felt compelled to remove a stone from the satanic circle in the lodge and left with it. I think he cursed himself when he did that. But it goes farther than that. A couple of years earlier, we were at the Hellfire Caves in England (which are connected to the Hellfire Lodge in Ireland), where a witch doused Aaron in goat's blood during a pagan ritual. He wasn't the same after that ceremony; I think he was toying with things that he wasn't prepared to deal with. His experience at the lodge was a combination of both events, not a singular event. He's a strong person, but no one is equipped to deal with the devil and his demons.

I've looked through his eyes and he's looked through mine.

A few nights later, we did our investigation at Loftus Hall, and Aaron still wasn't himself. I thought it was too soon for him to continue investigating, but he is too much of a professional not to go on. We had to let him participate for the sake of the show, but for me it was like being a corner man and telling your fighter that he can't fight anymore despite his broken hands and nose. His drive won't allow the injuries to hold him back, but you know that he's just in for more pain if he continues. At Loftus Hall I was using the structured light sensor camera, and a spirit appeared on Aaron's head while he was calling out to the devil. The spirit even did things on command while Aaron was in a near-catatonic state. I was torn because it was an incredible paranormal moment, but it was also forcing my friend even deeper into the darkness.

As I'm writing this chapter, we've been back from Ireland for only a few weeks, and Aaron's still not himself. He isn't losing his mind, but he's been quiet and secretive, and I don't know what's going on with him. We went to Ireland to find answers and debunk myths, but we came back freaked out like never before.

I can't say for certain that we found the devil himself, but as a scientist in the study of the paranormal, I observed a key element that I can't explain. I have no answer except to say that it's a little terrifying. Even if I was an utter skeptic, what I felt and saw is crazy, and I'm worried for Aaron. Maybe he'll be fine by the time this book comes out. Or maybe it will get worse. I don't know. I'm definitely concerned. To see what happened to him made me question why I do this a little bit. Some people have experiences with God and want them to last forever.

AND SOME UNFORTUNATE SOULS
HAVE EXPERIENCES WITH SATAN
AND DON'T WANT TO REMEMBER THEM.

35

NATIVE AMERICANS

Some cultures are more in tune with
the spirit world than others.

The paranormal is a fad right now. It's been booming for years because of movies and TV shows about the supernatural, social media that makes it easy for people who are interested in the paranormal to connect, and even iPhone apps that claim to enable anyone to be a paranormal investigator. Don't get me wrong; for the most part I'm not complaining. But like anything else, there are pros and cons to this rise in popularity. The paranormal has attracted a huge audience, so it's inevitable that people will want to get in and exploit it, even if they have no ability or background in the field. I see amateurs who want to get into the field all the time, and they all use the same approach: go high-tech. They think that they have to have suitcases full of cutting-edge technology to do the job. Although I like to use the latest equipment myself, I think there are low-tech strategies that work just as well. As I've said before, I believe in local and ancient rituals for getting in touch with the spirit world, and I feel that Native Americans are sadly overlooked when it comes to the search for answers about the afterlife.

Native peoples have been all over North America for more than 10,000 years. Long before European settlers set foot on the continent, indigenous tribes were here living in harmony with the natural environment and developing rituals centered around the sacredness of the Earth. I believe that to this day, Native Americans are more in tune with the Earth's energies than anyone else. And any paranormal researcher will tell you that there are energies radiating from the Earth, and that those energies likely interact with the afterworld and with the spirits.

We are surrounded by different types of energy. Geomagnetic and electromagnetic energy is everywhere, and some places, like Sedona, Arizona, are vortices of energy that may have healing powers for humans. We in the paranormal community believe that these vortices can even be portals to the other side. When you look at Native American culture, you see people who believe that wind, water, fire, and earth are primary forces emanating from the Creator and participate in rites centered around those forces. Some people find that silly, but not me. I think native peoples identify certain spots as sacred for a reason—they either know or feel something the rest of us don't.

When you look at some of the most well known and documented haunted sites in the world, they're frequently earthbound, like the Bell Witch Cave in Tennessee. It's said that the hauntings there were so powerful, the government tried to decipher what was happening and couldn't. Andrew Jackson himself studied it and couldn't explain its strange phenomenon, but here's the eerie part: The Bell Witch Cave lies beneath a Native American burial ground believed to be thousands of years old. The natives chose this spot because they believed that it was a portal to the other side.

The cave at Rathcroghan in Ireland is viewed the same way, and it's known that the ancient Druids used the area as a ritualistic gathering place and cemetery. I think that older peoples like these were in more tune with the Earth than we are now, and the rituals that have been passed down for thousands of years reveal a little bit of what they knew. We're not half as deep or spiritual as they were. We have technology and scientists, and I respect them, but I think that ancient peoples knew more than we do today about the forces of the Earth and how they interact with the spirit world.

Nopeming, which means "out in the woods" in the Ojibwa (Chippewa) language, is a sanitarium in Minnesota built on top of mineral springs to which the Ojibwa sent their sick and dying to heal. Now it's an insanely haunted building with a history of massive death from tuberculosis, but I can't help but think that the real cause of the paranormal activity there is the residual Indian energy. I spoke with an Ojibwa medicine man, who said that the spirits of his ancestors are all over the site. Another of the most active places I've ever been is the David Oman house in California, which is also rumored to have been built on ancient Indian burial grounds.

All of these "coincidences" are amazing to me, and I think we can learn a lot from Native Americans and their relationship with the Earth. They're largely a private people, but if you get a chance to speak with them, you can learn about a whole different dimension of spirituality. I think our focus on technology and gathering scientific data makes us overlook the low-tech ways of getting in touch with spirits. We may even be losing the true essence of spirituality by relying on gadgets.

NATIVE AMERICANS TURNED TO MOTHER NATURE LONG AGO FOR ANSWERS TO THE MYSTERIES OF LIFE. I BELIEVE SHE GAVE THEM SOME.

36

GO TO THE LIGHT

Freeing a spirit is not that easy.

If there's one criticism I get tired of hearing as a paranormal investigator, it's this: "You don't tell spirits to go to the light. You need to tell more spirits to go to the light." To me, this is more irritating than a pineapple enema.

The people who say this have been programmed by movies and TV shows that portray a false image of a psychic medium directing wayward spirits to move toward a bright white light that they somehow keep missing. I don't mean this as an attack on psychic mediums, but I keep hearing about mediums who use public forums and blogs to establish the presence of a mysterious light that spirits need to dive into to find peace. They have created this "go to the light" urban legend that the general public believes in and keeps reminding me to follow. People think psychic mediums are experts on freeing trapped spirits by giving them simple directions, which I just don't buy. It's not as easy as that.

The "go to the light" phenomenon has sparked a debate among groups within the paranormal community, but ultimately (and let me stress this) what happens when people die is *unknown*.

Only God knows what happens to us in the afterlife, and only He knows whether or not there's a spotlight that we're all required to step through. Based on hundreds of investigations and years of research, I have strong beliefs about it, but I could be completely wrong, and I admit that. And so could everyone else. Since it's nearly impossible to prove anything in this field, everything is a belief or a theory. But at least paranormal investigators like myself collect evidence, postulate theories, and try to test them through observation, trial, and error. Psychic mediums...not so much.

Don't get me wrong; I've known many psychic mediums, and I trust a few of them, especially Chris Fleming, Debby Constantino, and Michael and Marti Parry, whom I love working with. Real psychic mediums like these have a gift, a sense that I believe the rest of us lack. But not every psychic medium does. A lot of them are faking the funk and exaggerating their abilities. I'm not like that. I don't see spirits, and I damn sure don't tell people things like, "Someone whose name starts with the letter *P* is here in the room with us, and he's very happy to see you." That's either offering false hope or flat-out lying.

I believe that a lot of self-proclaimed psychic mediums do shotgun-blast readings to get a response. They go in front of a group of people and start mentioning letters or numbers and see who responds, knowing that someone will react. It's the law of averages (or Scamming 101) at work. If you throw out a series of random facts into a crowd, like, "Is there someone here who lost a father who smoked?" of course you will find someone who fits that description. The medium picks out a mark, and then it's a game of questions to pull the wool over everyone's eyes. It's a scam. I saw a clip of "Long Island Medium" Theresa Caputo on Anderson Cooper's show, where she did a shotgun-blast reading that went very badly.

No one was convinced, and even Cooper seemed disappointed. Can you say "karma"?

Like I said, this isn't an attack on psychic mediums, and I'm not saying that all of them are frauds, but there's a clear dividing line between the real ones and the fake ones. The fake ones always get caught, which is sweet justice, but still tragic for the field. They toy with emotionally traumatized people for profit and give the paranormal community a bad name. Picking out a stranger and opening up old wounds is wrong, especially when they say that they're making contact with a deceased family member. I don't think any of their exploits should be covered in the media as miracles or even success stories. There are good PMs and bad PMs, just like there are good PIs and bad PIs. The bad ones need to be called out and exposed, like Sylvia Browne was.

In 2003, Amanda Berry, a 16-year-old girl from Cleveland, went missing. Desperate for answers, Berry's family turned to Browne in 2004 for a spiritual answer on the Montel Williams show. What did Browne do? She told the family that Amanda was dead, and they gave up hope, even when the FBI said that she could still be alive. Berry's family believed Browne and cleaned out Amanda's room to put the memory of their daughter to rest. Then, in 2013, Amanda was found alive in the basement of Ariel Castro, with two other girls he'd held captive for more than ten years. Browne apologized, and the Berry family even forgave her, but in my eyes, Browne did a horrible thing.

When dealing with the relatives of people who have died, PMs shouldn't say a damn word about whether or not their family members have passed on to the next world, are happy or unhappy, or anything, really. It's wrong. And anyone who seeks out a medium should be prepared for pain. A bad PM will manipulate you until your wallet runs dry, so I strongly caution anyone thinking of consulting a *bad* psychic like Sylvia Browne. I do believe that there are gifted PMs, though. You just have to find the right one.

So back to going to the light. Ten times a week people ask me, "How come you never tell the spirits to go to the light?" Because I don't think it's true. Spirits are intelligent. You can't just tell them to go to the light and instantly free them from their painful purgatory and enable them to move on to the next world. You can't just say, "Go to the light," and spark an epiphany. The spirits don't just say, "Oh, you mean after forty years of wandering around this room, all I have to do is walk into that bright light that's been on this whole time? Damn!" I don't think that's how it works.

So instead of telling a spirit to go to the light, I try to connect and communicate. Every spirit has things to say. Spirits need to be heard and know that living people can hear them. That's how I believe they are freed. They don't need driving directions. They need to talk.

At Hill View Manor near Pittsburgh, I communicated with a spirit named Alicia. I was using the SB7 spirit box and asked, "What is your name?" She said, "Alicia." Then she said, "Can I ask you a question?" I said yeah. She said, "Let us...hear." I knew then that she wasn't at rest because she wanted someone to hear her voice and feel her pain. When she said the word *hear,* I could tell that she was crying or in complete sadness. This exchange of intelligent communication with the spirit of Alicia broke my heart, because I could feel her emotions transfer through me. As we shared that moment, only she and I truly understood its meaning for both of us. To this day, this is one of the most special moments I've had during intelligent interaction with a spirit.

We talked for a while, and eventually I could feel her move on. I could sense that she'd left the room, and I believe she passed on to another world. Did she go to heaven? I don't know, but she was

The Hill View Manor changed everything for the SB7 spirit box.

definitely gone, and I never told her to walk into a light. As an empath, I felt her emotions connect with mine in a way that no one else could ever comprehend. I wanted to cry, yet I felt something beautiful had happened because she found closure. She just needed someone like me to hear her and share her pain. My energy and that connection are what finally freed her. Talking to spirits is how you release them. Listening to them is how you help them cross over.

Think about it in terms of real life. If you're in a state of depression or pain, what helps you move on from that state? Talking it out. Sitting down with a psychologist, psychiatrist, friend, teammate, or whomever is therapy. People go to a support group to talk to other people about their problems because that's where the healing happens. We all have the gift of being able to heal people by talking to them, listening to their problems, and helping them get through them. People who care get on the same emotional wavelength with those who are suffering. People always say, "I'm on the same wavelength as this person," or, "I really made a connection with that person," during times of very good or very bad emotions. There's a reason for that. It's because people connect with other people.

That night at Hill View Manor, I was on the same emotional wavelength as Alicia. I could feel her sadness and was nearly in tears when we connected. That's how I helped her move on. She didn't move on because I said, "Hey, Alicia, go to the light." If it was that easy, we'd all walk around all day saying it. We'd all be healers, and the spirits would be like, "Cool…did it. Later." Then everyone could do this job, and trust me…

IT'S JUST NOT THAT EASY.

37

HATERS

We've all seen them: people who just can't stand to see other people succeed. It doesn't matter if you're a great actor accepting an Oscar or a great janitor accepting a Mopster, if you're good at what you do and get recognized for it, someone will hate you. After years of dealing with that kind of contempt, all I can say is, don't feed the trolls.

I've worked very hard to get where I am. I struggled for many years and had to keep my chin up when so many people told me that I had no future. I went through a lot of bad stuff before I finally found what I was passionate about and built a brand around it. *Ghost Adventures* connected me to a lot of people who are like me—obsessed with knowing more about the paranormal and helping those who have had unexplainable experiences cope with them. I'm not about to step aside from all that just because someone hates me. If you think I'm that weak, then you've seriously misjudged me.

When *Ghost Adventures* became a success, a lot of bad people tried to take my achievements away from me. They took notice of me and the size of my fan base and tried to bring me down. They were haters, bullies, and trolls with black hearts and no ethics. And a lot of people tried to get at the things I worked hard to earn while doing something I am passionate about. It really made jaded about people, I admit it.

Old acquaintances (notice I didn't say *friends*) tried to get things like money or fame, or wanted to use my fan base to promote every single thing they did, and got mad when I didn't provide them. I've worked hard for my success. Why do I owe them anything? Why do they try to take the things I've earned? I love my job for many reasons, but one big reason is that when I'm filming on location, I am free from society and the distasteful things that come with it. I get to get away and block out everything. I go to my island.

When I'm not filming *GA*, I'm at home living in the here and now, but it seems that the more successful my shows, albums, movies, and books are, the more people try to get at me and use me for my money. And they don't just try to steal what I have, but also what I've made. Copycat shows and books have popped up everywhere. I learned very quickly that the more creative you are, the more protective you have to be of your work.

Even within the paranormal community, there are haters who attack us. Their TV show failed after one season because they weren't passionate or knowledgeable enough to carry it, so they start shit with me, my crew, and our fans in order to feel important again. It's pathetic. They spread hate toward us when in reality they're unhappy with their own lives. We don't usually return the bashing, but sometimes I can't help myself. I say enough is enough (especially when the haters attack the fans) and return the barb. But in the end, all the squabbling really does is give the field a bad name. Paranormal investigation will never be taken seriously as a science if we play reindeer games. We're professionals, not actors hired to play them. We leave that to the other paranormal shows.

Everyone has a different reason for hating. Maybe someone got beaten to the punch by someone else in the same field. Maybe someone else was being considered for a role on a paranormal show when I came along and took it. Maybe they don't like my hair or the way I speak. Maybe they don't believe in ghosts and want to tear me down because I do. Maybe they are just plain jealous. You may not like what I do. You may not like me personally. You may not like the color black, and that's fine. I don't like clowns and avoid them at all costs, but I don't ridicule people who dress up as clowns and try to make kids smile at birthday parties and circuses. Everyone has their own reason for doing what they do; it's a personal thing that is part of them.

Haters actually help us in a way because they create buzz and get people talking about the show. The funny thing is, they stop chirping once you confront them. It's amazing how quickly people will back down when they come face-to-face with the person they hate. I used to get angry about haters, but that's what they want. They want to see you blow your top and go off on a photographer or autograph seeker while their buddies film it and then put it on Vine, Twitter, Facebook, YouTube, and every other media outlet they can in hopes that TMZ will pick it up and they will get famous themselves. How ironic is that?

To be honest, I don't understand why some people get so obsessed with hurting me that they spend their energy trying to tear me down. Am I that irritating, or do they just have nothing else whatsoever to do? I wish they'd take all that dedication and focus it into something positive, like cleaning up a beach or saving an abandoned animal.

The big drawback of being well known is that I can't give everyone my personal attention. I used to respond to everyone who wrote me, tweeted me, or whatever. But then my life turned into a *Cable*

If you live your life as a hater, go to Disneyland and grow up.

Guy movie. Once I gave the obsessive types some attention, they wouldn't leave me alone and ruined it for everyone else. People think I should be held to a different standard because I'm a TV show host, but I just can't do it. I can't come home from filming for three to five days and spend ten more hours a day on the computer answering messages from fans. I try to tweet out short responses to good questions, but I can't respond to everyone, especially when I'm asked the same questions over and over again. "Zak, what's your favorite investigation?" I get that one twenty times a day. Am I a typical entertainment guy who ignores his fans? No, but there simply aren't enough hours in the day for me to respond to every request. I'm sorry for that, but it's the unfortunate truth, and it breeds haters.

I love my fans to death, as long as they're not totally creepy like the ones I described in chapter 32, "Crazy Fans." My fans are the best people in the world, and I truly enjoy interacting with the ones who understand boundaries. But when they don't, it just makes me want to stay indoors, sharpen sticks, and wait for the end of the world. A fan once got too obsessed, and things went south very quickly to the point where I had to get a restraining order.

Haters also make it hard to determine whom to trust. When I meet someone for the first time, I can't tell whether they're genuinely interested in me and what I do or whether they just want something from me, like an invitation to be on the show or tickets to the next UFC fight (since I live in Vegas). I'm never sure who's telling me the truth and who's just telling me what they think I want to hear. Are people being fake so that they can be close to me, or are they being real? It's hard to tell sometimes. There are definitely people who act differently around me. They're usually more nervous than they should be, which is always a bad sign, and since I'm an empath I can feel it. Most people can't hide who they are around me.

So are you guilty of this yourself? Be honest. It's not an accusation, but a question. Have you gotten obsessed with a TV personality and wanted so badly to be around him or her that you sacrificed who you are? Or do you hate successful people and watch an unbeaten sports team just to see them lose? Do you watch Floyd Mayweather fight just so you can be there when someone finally dishes him a dose of failure and see the look on his face when he has to admit that he's not perfect? It's not weak to admit that you have these kinds of tendencies. In fact, if you do, then you're one step closer to knowing yourself, and that's much more important in life than you might think.

It's only human to want to see successful people fail, but I honestly don't. I've been there, and I know what it's like on this side of the velvet ropes. I've swum that river and climbed out onto the far shore a different person. I don't hate the successful people of the world; in fact, I want to see them succeed. If they're talented and work hard, then why hate them for it? Isn't that the piece of the American pie we all want so badly to eat?

All the haters out there need to know one great truth about me:

AS LONG AS THERE ARE ENOUGH PEOPLE
WHO LIKE WHAT I DO, I'LL CONTINUE
TO DEDICATE MYSELF TO THEM
AND LET THE REST STEW
IN THEIR OWN HATE.

38

WHEN I DIE

What's at the end of this train ride?

I've chosen a profession that forces me to have a close relationship with death and the afterlife, and I think about those things constantly. All the time. I never stop thinking, ever. And the deeper and deeper my journeys, experiences, and interactions with spirits get, the more I think about my own death. What will happen? I'm not in a rush to find out—I have a lot of living left to do—but still, it's intriguing to think about.

First, a quick detour. On November 6, 2014, I was in a Cadillac Escalade traveling to Goldfield Ghost Town in Arizona. We were driving along the base of Superstition Mountain, which is said to be steeped in curses and Native American lore. That probably had nothing to do with what was about to happen, but it's worth mentioning. Billy was driving, I was in the passenger seat, and Aaron and Jay were in the back. We came to a four-way intersection where we had a stop sign but the cross traffic did not. (This is important.) Billy stopped, but as he started through the intersection, I felt strangely compelled to lift my head from my phone and look to my right. What I saw scared the life out of me.

When Billy stopped at the stop sign, he did not look to his right to see a car barreling toward us at 55 mph, and proceeded to accelerate through the intersection like an idiot. When Billy is driving, Aaron's, Jay's, and my heads are usually bent down over our phones, but for some reason I lifted mine as I felt the car move from the stop sign, and that decision saved my life. I screamed at Billy to stop. The oncoming car, thinking we would stay stopped at the stop sign, saw us in the middle of the intersection, about to get T-boned. The car swerved around us, tires screeching and smoking on the asphalt, and nearly flipped. Then it crashed into the bushes and cactuses on the shoulder of our side of the road.

We sat there for a few seconds trying to absorb what the hell had just happened. I screamed at Billy. How could he not look to the right? If I hadn't lifted my head, this car would have T-boned us, smashing directly into my door, and I know I would have been killed. I was pissed, and I let Billy know it.

We went to the other car to check on the driver, an elderly gentleman who had only one arm. I think he had a veteran's hat on. He was in shock, just sitting there amid the smoke pouring from his car, speechless and unable to move. We all just stared at each other, knowing that Billy had nearly just caused some of us to be killed. We were literally within an inch of stepping through the door of the unknown while we were on our way to investigate the afterlife at the base of a cursed mountain. To make a long story short, I screamed at Billy hardcore, but an hour later we were already cracking jokes about it. Let's just say that when Billy drives now, I never look down at my phone.

At moments like this, I honestly feel that my life was predestined. After my first real experience with a spirit, which occurred when I was just a kid, I was chosen by some greater forces to do what I'm doing now. It's almost like I have spiritual strings attached to me, and at times those forces act as a puppeteer, leading me to have certain thoughts and go to certain places at certain times and reignite the energy there by bringing my own energy. I'm constantly being guided by spirits and other powerful forces in ways that defy rational explanation. They want me to reopen cold cases and stories that don't have proper endings. I feel like a spiritual missionary doing not God's work, but the work chosen by certain spirits.

At almost every location I investigate, I tend to have a deep experience that stays with me. I never have these experiences anywhere else, and they're getting stronger. Each experience is so powerful and emotional and beyond this living life that I feel like I am supposed to be there to make this connection. I feel like my energy is doing something beyond myself in these locations. It's fulfilling the needs of the spirits there, but sometimes the spirits are not all good, and I don't realize it until it's too late. I feel like I'm roaring down the tracks of a spiritual railway, and I can't get off no matter what I do. It makes me think about what's at the end of the line: my own death.

I believe that when my death comes, I will visit the locations I've investigated one more time. I believe that in the afterlife I'll travel to all the places where I've left a residue of my own energy. It's like having my own private doorway that I will walk through at each place. The journeys I'm taking now are training me for that time—for how I'm going to live my afterlife. It's soul training.

I never planned to get the tattoo on my left arm. I just woke up one day and decided I needed it. It says, "The dead travel fast." My other tat is of Vlad Tepes (better known as Dracula), whom I feel is a real vampire living past his first death. I experienced his spirit in Romania. During my White Rite ceremony in Paris, Father Sebastiaan told me that being a vampire is about living beyond your first death.

One thing scares the shit out of me when I think about crossing over and passing through those doorways: Are the spirits I've pissed off going to be there waiting for me? They could be, so I also train to build my spiritual armor. There are no textbooks or manuals that will prepare you for death (except the Bible), so I'm blazing my own trail. If you believe in it, you will spend an eternity with God in heaven. If not, who knows, but I'll be ready either way.

I feel like my body and soul are day and night. I'm constantly being driven one way and then pulled back the other. The cover of this book is a good illustration of that struggle. I've got demons, angels, and spirits fighting to pull me in different directions all the time. I wish I could give everyone a secret password to summon me when I pass over, like saying "Beetlejuice" three times. But if we could do that, then there would be phone booths set up to talk to the other side, or someone would make an app for your phone so you could call up your great-great-grandfather and ask how things went down at Gettysburg. There would be no mysteries in life. What fun would that be?

Living forms are more in tune with the world around us and the afterlife than we think. I've said before that I think the human body is a perfectly reliable detector of paranormal energy. Our minds are powerful, and our consciousness is amazing. The problem is that we're stuck in these bodies that decay and degrade over time, and we even help the process along by indulging in vices like drugs and alcohol and letting our minds get worn down by the stresses of relationships, work, bills, terrorism, religion, you name it. We don't channel our energy well. We're distracted by everything. We don't take the time to learn how to use our minds more fully.

At death, when life ends and all the trivial things of this world disappear, I believe that our minds are finally freed from all distractions, and we're allowed to focus singularly and freely on one thing. Some souls cross over into a realm we don't know about yet. Others turn their focus to something they hold dear, like a family member or a house to roam carefree. Our bodies have to stay in one physical place and time, but our spirits are free after death, and our consciousness takes on a new ability to do things. But we'll never know until we cross over.

I think death is a mystery that needs to remain somewhat secret. I like to poke and prod around it and try to get a glimpse of what happens when we cross over, but we won't (and shouldn't want to) know for sure until we step through that door one last time and learn what God has in store for us. That's how He made it, and I do believe in Him. I wasn't meant to die in a car crash in Arizona. I'm meant for something else.

IT'S ALL A DESIGN, AND IT ALL HAS MEANING.